13/17

EXPERIENCING BILLY JOEL

The Listener's Companion
Gregg Akkerman, Series Editor

Titles in **The Listener's Companion** provide readers with a deeper understanding of key musical genres and the work of major artists and composers. Aimed at nonspecialists, each volume explains in clear and accessible language how to *listen* to works from particular artists, composers, and genres. Looking at both the context in which the music first appeared and has since been heard, authors explore with readers the environments in which key musical works were written and performed.

EXPERIENCING BILLY JOEL

A Listener's Companion

Thomas MacFarlane

ROWMAN & LITTLEFIELD
Lanham • Boulder • New York • London

Published by Rowman & Littlefield
A wholly owned subsidiary of The Rowman & Littlefield Publishing Group,
Inc.
4501 Forbes Boulevard, Suite 200, Lanham, Maryland 20706
www.rowman.com

Unit A, Whitacre Mews, 26-34 Stannary Street, London SE11 4AB

British Library Cataloguing in Publication Information Available

Library of Congress Cataloging-in-Publication Data

Names: MacFarlane, Thomas, 1960– author.
Title: Experiencing Billy Joel : a listener's companion / Thomas MacFarlane.
Description: Lanham, MD : Rowman & Littlefield, 2016. | Series: The listener's companion |
Includes bibliographical references and index.
Identifiers: LCCN 2016011109 (print) | LCCN 2016012221 (ebook) | ISBN 9781442257689
(cloth : alk. paper) | ISBN 9781442257696 (electronic)
Subjects: LCSH: Joel, Billy–Criticism and interpretation. | Rock music–United States–History and
criticism.
Classification: LCC ML420.J72 M33 2016 (print) | LCC ML420.J72 (ebook) | DDC
782.42166092–dc23 LC record available at http://lccn.loc.gov/2016011109

Printed in the United States of America

For my grandfather, Denni Fuschi, who taught me about patience and strength. For my grandmother, Josephine Fuschi, who taught me about the joy of laughter. And finally, for their daughter Mary Jane, who in 1964 bought me my first Beatles albums and in the process taught me about the beauty of popular song.

CONTENTS

SERIES EDITOR'S FOREWORD

The goal of the Listener's Companion series is to give readers a deeper understanding of pivotal musical genres and the creative work of its iconic composers and performers. This is accomplished in an inclusive manner that does not require extensive music training or elitist shoulder rubbing. Authors of the series place the reader in specific listening experiences, in which the music is examined in its historical context with regard to both compositional and societal parameters. By positioning the reader in the real or supposed environment of the music's creation, the author provides for a deeper enjoyment and appreciation of the art form. Series authors, often drawing on their own expertise as both performers and scholars, deliver to readers a broad understanding of major musical genres and the achievements of artists within those genres as lived listening experiences.

The Listener's Companion series has several titles on rock and pop topics, but *Experiencing Billy Joel* is the first entry in the piano-vocalist genre. Joel has had thirty-three Top 40 hits in America with sales of over 150 million albums worldwide. His awards include induction to the Rock and Roll Hall of Fame (1999), the Kennedy Center Honors (2013), and five Grammy Awards. But if he had not created anything beyond "Piano Man," released in 1973, he would still have scored a huge success. The song only peaked at a modest number 28 on the U.S. pop charts in 1974, but has simply refused to fade away, eventually becoming Joel's signature piece and the bane of every piano-bar entertainer on the planet who is expected to play the song multiple times every night. Fortunately, Joel didn't stop with his first hit and has a songwriting career of the greatest depth and breadth. A smattering of his hits include "Just the Way You Are," "Uptown Girl," "It's Still Rock and Roll to Me," "She's Always a Woman," "Allentown," "We Didn't Start the Fire," "Leave a Tender Moment Alone," "Moving Out," "New York State of Mind," "She's Got a Way," and "You May Be Right." Joel is easily one of the most successful songwriters in history of American music.

Thomas MacFarlane's insight into the music of Billy Joel is staggering. Based on our communications during his writing of this book I can say that I have never met anyone with as much awareness of Joel's musical output. I am particularly impressed with MacFarlane's ability to place the music of Joel into the context of the times, both in regard to changes in the music industry and Joel's personal life. Our awareness of Joel may have begun with "Piano Man," but MacFarlane walks us through the many phases of the songwriter's catalog with the kind of non-jargon writing style that is just perfect for the Listener's Companion.

Gregg Akkerman

PREFACE

The Girl on the Train (December 14, 1978)

$\mathbf{S}$inger-songwriter Billy Joel remains one of the most acclaimed and celebrated popular musicians of our time. More than four decades after the release of his signature song, "Piano Man" (1973), his work continues to appeal to new generations of listeners not yet born when he first appeared on the scene. Compared to many of his musical contemporaries, it's clear that Joel's standard has remained remarkably high. The eclectic nature of his work points to an innate curiosity regarding the potential of popular song and its connections with the musical and artistic traditions of the past. Although arguably not a producer/composer in the modern sense, his habit of developing compositions in the studio and writing entire albums as unified statements does suggest an ongoing interest in the aesthetics of recorded sound.

Over the course of his career, Billy Joel released a series of remarkable albums that charted an artist's journey from obscurity to international success. *Experiencing Billy Joel: A Listener's Companion* is an exploration of that journey. Following an overview of his emergence from the Long Island music scene, this book will provide selected analyses for each of Joel's twelve pop albums, designed to appeal to musicians and non-musicians alike.

In earlier studies, I adapted the eclectic method of analysis developed by Dr. Lawrence Ferrara in the book, *Philosophy and the Analysis of Music* (1991). This method allowed for an effective engagement of compositional form, referential meaning, and musical sound. My adaptations of Ferrara's method attempted to focus his approach on the peculiar aesthetics of multi-track recordings. *Experiencing Billy Joel: A Listener's Companion* features a more casual, less systematic discussion that is, nevertheless, informed by those earlier studies. In addition to engaging Joel's works in terms of their various texts and musical settings, this book will also explore the distinctive qualities of the production styles that characterized his development as a recording artist.

For the most part, I have opted to discuss the lyrics first since Billy Joel typically begins with music and then paints his melodies with text. Thus, in terms of the direction of process, I will start with the surface and work my way back toward the compositional center. I should also point out that the song choices made here, as well as the readings of those choices, are not intended to be definitive. The reader is encouraged to disagree and develop his or her own take on the material. Ultimately, the goal is to generate conversation into how Billy Joel's recorded works combine to create the foundation for a complex and enduring musical legacy.

In the following section I will, with the reader's permission, provide a firsthand account of Billy Joel's emergence as a solo artist during the 1970s. This account will seek to engage with the reasons Joel's music made perfect sense to the listeners of that time. The goal is to provide a measure of context and to create a narrative based on personal experience that works as a kind of fractal of cultural history.

✵ ✵ ✵

In his book, *Sex, Drugs, and Cocoa Puffs: A Low Culture Manifesto*, author Chuck Klosterman writes, "[Billy] Joel is the only rock star I've ever loved who I never wanted to be . . . Every one of Joel's important songs—including the happy ones—are ultimately about loneliness."[1] Unlike Klosterman, I must admit that in my younger days, I actually wanted to *be* Billy Joel. He was the prototype, the one who had made it all happen. For music students like me, Joel was the validation of everything we'd been hearing and somehow wanted to become.

It was just before Christmas and I was on my way to see Joel's opening night at the Madison Square Garden. When I say "opening night," I really do mean, *opening night*. He had been touring regularly since the early 1970s, but this would be his first gig at New York's premier pop music venue.[2] His recent albums, *The Stranger* (1977) and *52nd Street* (1978), had put him firmly atop the pop world, and the legend of his success was pervading the entire culture. The Stranger, it seems, had now become the celebrated native son.

As a pianist, I'd been playing Joel's songs for years and knew that somehow, someway, I had to get to that concert. My outfit for the occasion was based on the cover photo from the album *52nd Street*: suit jacket with dress shirt and tie over blue jeans and white sneakers. At the time, this fashion statement made perfect sense as a blend of middle-class prepster with finger-snapping beatnik: conformity meeting rebelliousness head-on. It also seemed to reach across to the Chaplinesque wardrobe of Diane Keaton in the film *Annie Hall* (1977). Thus, my ensemble could perhaps be seen as a kind of cross-dressing in reverse.

Professor Emile DeCosmo, my tutor in jazz improvisation, allowed me to leave class early so that I'd have enough time to get to the Garden. Between the local bus and the train, I somehow managed to make it on time, buy a ticket from a scalper, and take my seat in the upper level. The show itself was exciting and very musical and seemed to touch on all the things that got me into Billy Joel in the first place: strong, sweeping melodies, complex chord progressions, and jazz/blues flourishes in the overall approach. I was especially impressed with "Root Beer Rag," since it demonstrated Billy Joel's virtuosic abilities at the piano.

Afterward, I took the PATH train back home to New Jersey. My particular train car was empty, but when we stopped at the 14th Street station, an attractive young lady got on board. She had dark brown hair, green eyes, and was wearing an elegant belted raincoat coat topped off with a Joni Mitchell/Rickie Lee Jones–style beret. She also carried a black leather backpack that she positioned awkwardly on her knee. The occasion demanded that I work up the nerve to talk to her. The only problem was that she seemed to be in her mid-twenties, while I was only eighteen. Luckily, my shirt and tie made me look a bit older, or so I thought.

I had spent the previous few years studying at Rea's Music, a neighborhood music shop that rebuilt, sold, and tuned all manner of acoustic pianos and also offered private lessons. There may be a piano shop on the Left Bank in Paris, but Rea's was conveniently located in Bayonne,

New Jersey, just around the corner from my house.[3] Rea's also featured an impressive collection of sheet music. Following my weekly lesson, I would often linger at their display case browsing through various transcriptions of songs that I had heard both on radio and television. Along with the most recent Top 10 hits, curios such as "Casino Royale," "Goodbye, Columbus," and "Remembering You" were all prominently on display.[4]

Years later, I would look back on my teenage years as a kind of extended waiting room, and much of that waiting took place at Rea's. As my teen years dragged on, I grew weary of the creeping rock 'n' roll hangover. In an effort to fight off this malaise, I began to explore the exotic chordal harmonies of jazz. In the early 1970s, innovative artists like Chick Corea and Herbie Hancock had been attempting to bridge the gap between jazz and rock, and soon, pop artists like Joni Mitchell, Paul Simon, Steely Dan, and Stevie Wonder all began to follow suit. Expansive harmonic structures and complex textures were now becoming the norm rather than the exception in pop music.

Back on the PATH train, I walked across the car, introduced myself to the girl, and sat down. During our conversation, I learned that she was twenty-three and a piano student in the graduate division at Mannes College.[5] I also learned that her name was Victoria. She was even prettier up close than she'd been at a distance. I thought she might be coming from class, but she said that she'd been practicing for a recital she was planning to give over the winter break.

At this point, I had been studying classical piano to improve my technique, but compared to Victoria, I was clearly a novice. She took some scores out of her shiny backpack to show me what she was working on and I was suitably impressed by the difficulty of the pieces in her repertoire. She then asked what I was working on, so I showed her my copy of *The Real Book* and some of the charts from that evening's jazz improv class. As I did, I became conscious of the gap that existed between my jazz-derived sensibility and her more traditional, conservatory-based approach. She perused the various charts and then said, "Ah, jazz. I see you're more of a chord player."

There was something disquieting about that comment, but she was pretty, so I let it pass. She then asked where I was coming from, and finally, I had my chance. I was only a kid, but had just come from the biggest show in town. With all of her classical training, it seemed certain that the pianism of Billy Joel would impress her.

"I just came from the concert at Madison Square Garden," I said.

"Who was playing?" she asked.

"Billy Joel," I replied.

You see, at the piano shop, Billy Joel was considered the "musician's musician." He was a very skilled songwriter with an awareness of the history of popular song; he was also an accomplished, classically trained pianist with a natural flair for blues and jazz; finally, he was a gifted vocalist who could move easily between ballads and straight rock 'n' roll. Seated behind a piano, he could never be as authentic or as sexy as your average pop star, but he did have an edge to his performance style that would ultimately help him transcend the limitations of "rock." In the early '70s, Joel had emerged from the suburban wilderness of Long Island to become a one-man version of the Beatles. Barely out of his teens, he was writing and recording entire albums of original material that easily matched the best work of the era.

Like many listeners, my first exposure to Billy Joel's music was through the 45 rpm single "Piano Man," released in late 1973. That year, the radio was teeming with songs that featured keyboard as the lead instrument, and Joel's contribution was a Dylanesque pop ballad that read like a folk-pop version of "Desolation Row." The prominent harmonica line certainly suggested homage, but the lyrics were different. They had a unique painterly quality that seemed more connected to Edward Hopper than to Bob Dylan. "Piano Man" was a great boost to pianists everywhere, but I was more impressed by the B-side, "You're My Home," a song that featured a confident sustained note sung by Joel during the fadeout. "Wow!" I thought to myself, "this guy can *really* sing!"

One morning during my senior year, a radio deejay announced the release of a single from Billy Joel's new album, *The Stranger*. The song was called "Just the Way You Are," and I noticed that it began with the same distinctive keyboard sound that had been featured on "Still Crazy after All These Years" by Paul Simon, released two years earlier.[6] As I had done with Simon's album, I soon learned all the songs from *The Stranger* and then began to move systematically through Billy Joel's previous works. Before long, I could play his entire catalog and demonstrated this feat at a series of recitals hosted by my teacher that year.

Encouraged by the reception to those performances, I decided to become a piano major, which leads us back to the girl on the train. . . .

After I told Victoria whose concert I had seen at the Garden, there was a long and somewhat awkward pause. I thought Billy Joel would impress her, but she seemed rather tense and reluctant to respond. In the window behind her, I watched the lights on the tunnel wall moving quickly in rhythm. Finally, she spoke.

"Billy Joel—I don't like him," she said.

"You don't like him?" I replied.

"No, not at all," she said.

I was stunned. This was the first time that I'd ever heard anyone express an unequivocal disdain for Joel.

"Why not? I mean, why don't you like him?" I struggled.

"Well, I suppose he's a decent musician. He seems to play the piano well enough, but why does he use all those oddly dissonant cluster chords? They don't seem necessary at all. In fact, they just slow things down."

Victoria was referring here to the jazz-derived harmonies that Joel blended with his more classically driven compositional forms.

"Also, I have a real problem with his lyrics," she continued.

"His lyrics? What's wrong with his lyrics?" I stammered.

"Well, he's always telling you what you should be doing in your life. He always seems to want to give you advice on what you need to change in order to be happy," she said.

I tried to get a handle on what Victoria was saying. As she spoke, I raced back through various Billy Joel song lyrics to try to find examples. His albums featured a good number of songs that tended to create vivid character sketches, but I began to see what it was she was getting at. Joel would sometimes use those characters as the springboard for making recommendations to his listeners. It never bothered me before, but I could see what she meant.

She continued, "It's not that big a deal, because it's only pop music, right? But, I really don't need someone to tell me what to do. I mean, how does he know what I need?"

She seemed so sure of herself. I didn't know what else to say. At that point, I'd never heard a discouraging word about the man or his music. Following another lengthy and awkward pause, Victoria asked, "So then, what do you like about Billy Joel?"

I've been trying to come up with a suitable answer to this question ever since. . . .

ACKNOWLEDGMENTS

I would like to extend my grateful appreciation to the following scholars and practitioners, whose kind encouragement contributed to the completion of this book: Gregg Akkerman, Rhys Clark, Emile DeCosmo, Joshua Duchan, David Elliott, Don Evans, Lawrence Ferrara, Phil Galdston, John Gilbert, Bennett Graff, Lara Graham, Olivier Julien, Graham MacFarlane, Ryan Madora, Dominick Maita, Natalie Mandziuk, Arthur Marino, David Matthews, Panos Mavromatis, Ira Newborn, Robert Rowe, Alex Ruthmann, Ron Sadoff, and Elise Sobol. The following friends and colleagues must also be acknowledged for their astute observations and helpful feedback: Ingrid Green, Paul Horan, and Mark Suozzo.

TIMELINE

February 15, 1922	Rosalind Nyman is born in New York City, United States.
June 12, 1923	Helmuth Julius (Howard) Joel is born in Nuremberg, Middle Franconia, Bavaria, Germany.
1942	Howard Joel immigrates with his parents to the United States.
1946	Howard Joel and Rosalind Nyman are married.
May 9, 1949	William Martin (Billy) Joel is born in the Bronx, New York, to Rosalind Nyman and Howard Joel.
1953	At the age of four, Billy Joel begins to show interest in music and is taken to study with a local piano teacher.
1957	Rosalind and Howard Joel divorce.
1964	As a teenager, Joel plays piano on the demo versions of "Leader of the Pack" and "Remember (Walking in the Sand)" by the Shangri-Las. According to producer Shadow Morton, Joel's part survives on the opening of "Remember (Walking in the Sand)."

February 9, 1964   Joel finds his vocation after watching the Beatles' first appearance on American television, on *The Ed Sullivan Show.*

1965   Joel joins a local group called the Echoes. The band will later change their name to the Emeralds and then, the Lost Souls. As the Lost Souls, the group will record "My Journey's End," an original song by Billy Joel.

1966–1969   Joel leaves the Lost Souls and begins to perform with a Long Island group, the Hassles, as keyboardist, songwriter, and vocalist. The Hassles record two albums for United Artists, which feature many original songs composed and performed by Billy Joel.

1969–1970   Joel forms the power duo Attila with Hassles bandmate Jon Small. Together, they release one album on Epic Records.

1971   Joel is signed to a contract with Family Productions and records *Cold Spring Harbor.* Sessions for the album take place at Record Plant Studios, Los Angeles, in July 1971. Several tracks on the final release were recorded earlier at Ultrasonic Recording Studios, Hempstead, New York.

November 1, 1971   Family Productions releases Joel's solo debut, *Cold Spring Harbor*, produced by Artie Ripp and arranged by Jimmie Haskell.

April 15, 1972   Billy Joel performs live on WMMR in Philadelphia as part of the tour to promote *Cold Spring Harbor.* He plays for a live audience at Sigma Sound Studios with his band: Rhys Clark (drums), Al Hertzberg (guitars), and Larry Russell (bass guitar). During the concert, the band performs a new song called "Captain Jack." The live recording of that song soon becomes the most

	requested track in the station's history and garners the attention of Columbia Records.
September 1973	Joel marries Elizabeth Weber Small.
September 1973	Sessions for the album *Piano Man* take place at Devonshire Sound, Los Angeles.
November 9, 1973	Family Productions/Columbia Records release *Piano Man*, produced by Michael Stewart and arranged by Michael Omartian.
1974	During the spring and summer months, sessions for the *Streetlife Serenade* album take place at Devonshire Sound, Los Angeles.
October 11, 1974	Family Productions/Columbia Records release *Streetlife Serenade*, produced by Michael Stewart and arranged by Michael Stewart and Billy Joel.
January 1976	Sessions for the *Turnstiles* album take place at Ultrasonic Recording Studios, Hempstead, New York.
May 19, 1976	Family Productions/Columbia Records release *Turnstiles*, produced by Billy Joel.
July–August 1977	Sessions for the album *The Stranger* take place at A&R Recording, Inc., 799 Seventh Avenue, New York City.
September 29, 1977	Family Productions/Columbia Records release *The Stranger*, produced by Phil Ramone.
July–August 1978	Sessions for the album *52nd Street* take place at A&R Recording, Inc., 799 7th Avenue at 52nd Street, New York City.
October 13, 1978	Family Productions/Columbia Records release *52nd Street*, produced by Phil Ramone.
1979–1980	Sessions for the album *Glass Houses* take place at A&R Recording, Inc., 799 Seventh Avenue, New York City.
March 10, 1980	Family Productions/Columbia Records release *Glass Houses,* produced by Phil Ramone.

June–July 1980	During the tour for *Glass Houses*, a series of live recordings are made for what is to become *Songs in the Attic*.
September 14, 1981	Family Productions/Columbia Records release the live album *Songs in the Attic*.
Spring 1982	Sessions for the album *The Nylon Curtain* take place at A&R Recording and Media Sound Studios, New York City.
July 20, 1982	Billy and Elizabeth Joel divorce.
September 23, 1982	Family Productions/Columbia Records release *The Nylon Curtain*.
Spring 1983	Sessions for the album *An Innocent Man* take place at Chelsea Sound and A&R Recording, Inc., New York City.
August 8, 1983	Family Productions/Columbia Records release *An Innocent Man*, produced by Phil Ramone.
December 1983	Columbia Records releases a remixed version of Billy Joel's first solo album, *Cold Spring Harbor* (1971), created by producer Artie Ripp. This new version is an attempt to correct the mastering errors that marred the album's original release. In the process, several tracks are re-edited by Ripp and drastically shortened from their original length.
March 1985	Billy Joel marries Christie Brinkley.
September 2, 1985	Family Productions/Columbia Records release Joel's collection, *Greatest Hits Volume I & Volume II*, produced by Michael Stewart, Billy Joel, and Phil Ramone.
December 29, 1985	Christie Brinkley gives birth to Alexa Ray Joel.
1985–1986	Sessions for the album *The Bridge* take place at the Power Station, Chelsea Sound (North), RCA Studios, New York City; and Evergreen Studios, Burbank, California.

July 29, 1986	Family Productions/Columbia Records release *The Bridge.*
Summer 1987	Joel gives a series of concerts in the Soviet Union. The shows are recorded for inclusion on the live album *Концерт.*
October 26, 1987	Sony BMG releases *Концерт.*
1988–1989	Sessions for the album *Storm Front* take place at the Hit Factory Times Square Studio, New York City; Right Track Recording, New York City; The Warehouse Studio, Vancouver, British Columbia; the Power Station, New York City.
October 17, 1989	Columbia Records releases *Storm Front*, produced by Mick Jones and Billy Joel.
1992	Billy Joel is belatedly awarded his diploma from Hicksville High School, 1967.
1993	Sessions for the album *River of Dreams* take place at the Boathouse at the Island Boatyard, Shelter Island, New York; Cove City Sound Studios, Glen Cove, New York; and the Hit Factory, New York City.
August 10, 1993	Columbia Records releases Joel's final new album of original songs, *River of Dreams,* produced by Billy Joel, Danny Kortchmar, Joe Nicolo, and David Thoener.
August 25, 1994	Billy Joel and Christie Brinkley divorce.
August 19, 1997	Columbia Records releases the collection *Greatest Hits Volume III*, produced by Phil Ramone, Mick Jones, Billy Joel, Danny Kortchmar, Joe Nicolo, and David Thoener.
June 1999	Sessions for the album *Fantasies & Delusions* initially take place at Cove City Sound Studios, Glen Cove, New York. However, the material is later re-recorded in Vienna, Austria.
May 2, 2000	Sony releases the live album *2000 Years: The Millennium Concert.*

December 20, 2000	Sony/Columbia releases the compilation titled *The Ultimate Collection*.
October 2, 2001	Sony Classical, Columbia releases Joel's collection of original classical works, titled *Fantasies & Delusions*, performed by pianist Richard Joo and produced by Steve Epstein.
October 2, 2001	Sony BMG releases *The Ultimate Collection*.
October 2, 2004	Billy Joel marries Katie Lee.
November 15, 2004	Columbia releases the compilation *Piano Man: The Very Best of Billy Joel*.
November 22, 2005	Sony BMG releases the box set compilation *My Lives*, which features rare tracks, alternate mixes, and previously unreleased songs that span Joel's entire professional career.
June 13, 2006	Columbia Records releases the live compilation *12 Gardens Live*.
June 2009	Billy Joel and Katie Lee Joel separate and later divorce.
November 16, 2010	Columbia Records releases the compilation *Billy Joel—The Hits*.
March 8, 2011	Helmuth Julius Joel dies in Vienna, Austria.
March 8, 2011	Columbia Records releases the album *Live at Shea Stadium: The Concert*, recorded July 16 and 18, 2008.
December 29, 2013	Billy Joel receives the Kennedy Center Honors.
July 13, 2014	Rosalind Nyman Joel dies at the age of ninety-two.
November 2014	Billy Joel becomes the sixth recipient of the Gershwin Prize for Popular Song.
July 4, 2015	Billy Joel marries Alexis Roderick.
August 12, 2015	Alexis Roderick gives birth to Della Rose Joel.

I

A PORTRAIT OF THE ARTIST

William Martin Joel had the good sense to be born to musical parents. Helmuth (Howard) Joel was a classically trained pianist who emigrated from Germany in the late 1930s, while Rosalind Nyman was a talented singer whose family hailed from Brooklyn, New York. The two were married in 1946 and moved up to the Bronx, where Billy Joel was born on May 9, 1949. The following year, the family resettled in the greener pastures of Hicksville, Long Island. Following this move, they adopted Rosalind's niece Judy, whose mother had recently passed away.[1]

Before long, young Billy began to exhibit a precocious musical talent that seemed to foreshadow his flair for composition. During an appearance on the television program, *Inside the Actors Studio* Joel described how, as a toddler, he would gently play a series of notes in the upper register of the piano. The resulting sounds seemed to suggest the gentle patter of rainfall. He would then repeat this process several more times. Finally, he would bash out a cluster of dissonant notes in the piano's lowest register in an emulation of thunder. Thus, Billy Joel's earliest known composition, "The Storm Song," was born.[2]

Fed up with her son's sonic experimentation, Rosalind Joel soon took the four-year-old Billy to his first formal piano lessons with Miss Frances, the local music (and ballet) teacher.[3] He showed a remarkable aptitude for the instrument, but like most children, he was not fond of practicing. In order to avoid learning pieces in their entirety, he would continue to develop his flair for composition:

My mother would be listening for me to practice a Mozart piece and rather than play the dots, I would just make up something in the style of Mozart . . . she would listen and she would go, "Oh, that's pretty good, you're learning that very quickly." And I'd say, "Yeah, this is easy." And then the next day, I wouldn't remember what I'd played the day before, so I'd play something different, but in the style of Mozart. And she'd go, "Oh, what's that?" And I'd go, "Oh, it's the second movement."[4]

Billy Joel suffered his first serious trauma when his parents divorced in 1957. Reportedly, Howard Joel had great difficulty adjusting to life in America and longed to return to the more traditional culture and values he'd left behind in Europe.[5] Following her husband's departure, Rosalind, who to this point had been a stay-at-home wife and mother, had to find a way to support the children. She found work where she could and came to depend increasingly on her relatives to look after Billy and his adopted sister Judy.[6]

Joel's maternal grandfather, Philip Nyman, provided a positive influence during this difficult time. Interestingly, he was something of a free spirit, and encouraged an independence of mind in the young Billy. Nyman was also cultured and well read, and tried to pass these interests on to his grandchildren, as Joel points out: "He didn't have a lot of money . . . but he would sneak us into the Brooklyn Academy of Music, by slipping the usher a pack of Luckies [Lucky Strikes] to see recitals and other classical music performances."[7]

Joel continued to study piano and soon developed an impressive technique. The word gradually got around about the boy from Hicksville who could play the piano like a pro. Jim Bosse, a high school friend and later a colleague in the Echoes, described Joel as having "an inner self-confidence that was unusual. We were fourteen, fifteen years old at the time. And his skills on piano were head and shoulders above where we were at that moment."[8]

In the early 1960s, Ira Newborn was introduced to Billy Joel through a family friend. Newborn would later go on to a brilliant career in film music, but at this point he was a young guitarist honing his craft. At their first meeting in Hicksville, he took note of Joel's advanced piano skills as well as his precocious knack for music composition:

So anyway, I'm there with Billy. I've brought the *Fake Book* and placed it on the piano. He begins to play from the book, and I'm playing guitar . . . Once, when he left the room to get something, I sat down at the piano to pick out a tune. It was then that I noticed that a lot of the hammers were broken. When Billy was playing, you couldn't hear that they were broken. He took note of which keys wouldn't play and avoided them. I was fourteen or fifteen at the time and I thought that this was very impressive. He also played me a few songs that he'd written, which was also impressive because they were really good. I'd never heard anyone that age composing and playing that well.[9]

INTERLUDE: BILLY JOEL AND THE BEATLES

According to Billy Joel himself, he ultimately decided to become a professional musician after seeing the Beatles perform on American television on February 9, 1964.[10] On that date, the group appeared on a weekly variety program called *The Ed Sullivan Show*, a broadcast that exposed them to approximately 73 million viewers nationwide.[11] For Joel, the group's unpolished personae and rebellious attitude made a lasting impression: "I thought, 'these guys don't look like Fabian. They don't look like they were manufactured in Hollywood' . . . I would see this look in John Lennon's eyes that told me something. They were irreverent, a bunch of wise guys like me and my friends!"[12]

As was the case for so many artists that arrived in their wake, the Beatles were a gift that kept on giving. In seven short years, the band created a remarkable catalog of songs and recordings that work together as a complete artistic statement. In the process, the Beatles revealed rock 'n' roll's potential to evolve into a viable popular art form. We're still trying to find an appropriate way to talk about the scope of their achievements. As we'll see in upcoming chapters, Billy Joel frequently returned to the band's standard and influence as a model for fostering the development of his own work.

At the same time, we should also point out that the Beatles could be a burden if a musician was not prepared to deal with the group's influence in an integrated fashion. In his book, *At the Apple's Core: The Beatles from the Inside*, film producer and Beatles collaborator Denis O'Dell writes:

It is a shame that so many contemporary British bands seem to use the Beatles as their main influence in their compositions and production, constantly trying to recreate the acid-soaked sound of Revolver-era Beatles. What is the point? With the "White Album" the Beatles proved their ability to look beyond their own immediate rock-and-roll heritage, and modern pop, if it is to progress with integrity, needs to do the same. In fact, if anything, slavish copying of the Beatles' music and image is, in a way, the most misguided tribute to them imaginable, since it represents everything they were not about. [13]

As O'Dell points out, a number of artists that followed the Beatles erred in their attempts to emulate the group's sound. The quality of that sound was something that the Beatles had inherited. It was a part of their own cultural identity and a by-product of the state of popular music when they first emerged onto the scene. Thus, attempts to emulate that sound would tend to result in a perceived lack of authenticity. Following O'Dell's reasoning, what these groups should have been trying to emulate was the kind of mind-set and openness that allowed the Beatles to make a *White Album*.

Billy Joel, though never secretive about his admiration for the Beatles, was among the few that did not seem particularly burdened by the band's sound. Over the course of his career, he tended to blend their influence with a variety of others. This musical alchemy resulted in a unique and highly original compositional voice. In a sense, his ability to blend different musical influences is what gives his work its considerable energy. Although he is often tagged as being McCartneyesque in his approach, Joel was actually more intrigued and ultimately inspired by the concise artistry of John Lennon, as he himself points out:

John Lennon had full awareness of the musical history. He had studied it all, and said early on that you can do a whole lot in a two- or three-minute rock song, that it was an art form in its own right . . . I think you have to have a good amount of innocence, ambition, and also confidence in your craft to be able to say, "We can tie all this up in three minutes." [14]

Though still a teenager, Joel's reputation as a musician continued to grow. By now, he had been studying classical piano for ten years and had developed a versatility that was the envy of the average musician.

As a result, he was asked to take part in the production of two of the most iconic pop songs of the 1960s: "Leader of the Pack," and "Remember (Walkin' in the Sand):

> It was 1964 and I was fourteen years old, and the guy producing the sessions for Red Bird Records was named Shadow Morton. I was asked to play piano on these two songs, "Remember (Walkin' in the Sand)" and "Leader of the Pack." . . . There were no singers at the time, and whether I cut a demo or the final master, I don't know, but I played on the recordings of those two songs, never got paid, and I was thrilled to even be in a professional recording situation.[15]

The coproducer of "Remember (Walkin' in the Sand)" was a man who would soon play a pivotal role in Joel's career: Artie Ripp.[16]

In 1965, Joel joined a local group called the Echoes. Soon, the Echoes would change their name to the Emeralds and then finally, the Lost Souls. As the Lost Souls, the group recorded an original Billy Joel composition titled "My Journey's End," which remained unreleased until it appeared on the collection *My Lives* in 2005. Although the song is a somewhat lackluster reworking of early '60s pop, there is an undeniable charm to the performance. Ultimately, its significance may lie in the way it reveals a young composer grappling with musical form.

In 1967, Billy Joel became the keyboardist and co–lead singer of the Hassles, a Long Island ensemble that emulated the sound and spirit of the Rascals. The group was signed to United Artists and recorded two albums, *The Hassles* (1967) and *Hour of the Wolf* (1969). In addition to handling lead vocals and keyboards, Billy Joel also wrote or cowrote most of the group's material. One of the most notable of these was "Hotel St. George," a charming and eccentric track from *Hour of the Wolf* that successfully echoes the psychedelic imagery of *Sgt. Pepper's Lonely Hearts Club Band.* Unable to make any headway on the charts, the Hassles disbanded in 1969.[17]

Billy Joel and former Hassles drummer Jon Small then created a heavy metal power duo called Attila, which was marked by a massive wall of sound. While Small provided a passionate beat on his drum kit, Joel played a Hammond B-3 that was wired into a stack of guitar amplifiers. He also used a small keyboard that allowed him to play bass lines in the manner of the Doors' Ray Manzarek. The duo's inspiration seems to have come primarily from organist Lee Michaels as well as late

'60s rock ensembles like Vanilla Fudge or the Zombies. They recorded one unsuccessful album for Epic Records before disbanding in 1970.[18]

COLD SPRING HARBOR (1971)

Overview

Following the breakup of the Hassles and the subsequent failure of Attila, Billy Joel found himself at a crossroads. With his teenage years behind him, his dreams of being a successful rock star were getting increasingly remote. He clearly had the talent to make a living as a musician, but where, and how? After a period of personal anguish that ultimately led to a failed suicide attempt, he concluded that the best course of action was to abandon his dreams of rock stardom and concentrate on songwriting. He now began to envision himself in the mold of Jimmy Webb, an American songwriter whose reputation was built on the success that others had with his remarkable compositions. Thus began the process that led to Billy Joel's debut solo release, *Cold Spring Harbor* (1971).[19]

Irwin Mazur, Joel's manager at the time, supported his decision to focus on songwriting. However, he also made it clear that if Billy really wanted his songs to be heard and recorded, he would have to make an album. Mazur then brokered a deal with Artie Ripp's Family Productions to get Joel's songs published and recorded.[20] Ripp was very impressed by Joel's demos, and was remarkably prescient in his assessment of the young artist's talent and potential:

> This is somebody who will be an important talent, that the world would say, "I love this guy!" He wrote a unique kind of lyric. His poetry and his reflection upon life and the life experience—he wasn't just writing "I love you, you love me, let's go play on the corner." He was really writing like a painter, a poet, a playwright. He engaged me. That was enough.[21]

By the time he came to work with Billy Joel, Artie Ripp had already achieved a certain stature as the director and cofounder of a production company that would later evolve into Kama Sutra Records.[22] After several years of success in the industry, Ripp moved to the West Coast and formed Family Productions, a label that would operate under the aegis of Paramount Records. Inspired by the work of Lou Adler, who'd just had a major hit with Carole King's *Tapestry*, Ripp began to move increasingly toward record production. His first major project in this regard was *Cold Spring Harbor*.[23]

The young Billy Joel was suitably impressed at the prospect of a deal with Artie Ripp. Following his experience with the Hassles and Attila, it must have seemed like a golden opportunity to work with someone who had a good track record in the business and who could plug him into the system. According to drummer Rhys Clark, Joel "was very excited about coming to L.A., and was looking forward to getting together with this producer to do an album. It seemed that it was a rather big break for someone so young, and he was very enthusiastic about it."[24]

The *Cold Spring Harbor* project began with a series of seven tracks/ demos intended for other artists and was recorded at Ultrasonic Recording Studios in Hempstead, New York. These were created under the auspices of Michael Lang, cocreator of the Woodstock festival, as Joel points out:

> I signed with a small company in New York called Just Sunshine which was run by Michael Lang, who did the Woodstock Festival, and as part of a deal that he had with Artie Ripp I got transferred to his label. I also signed all my publishing away, and I signed myself into a terrible deal. I was a dumb kid, and I would sign whatever I was told to sign. I was only about 20 and it's so easy to take advantage of a musician. I didn't know what was going on . . . I didn't know anything about publishing or monies that were owed to me. I found I got ripped off a lot while I was making the album.[25]

Two of these previously recorded tracks did survive onto the finished LP: "Why Judy Why," an acoustic ballad in the classic Beatles style; and "You Look So Good to Me," a catchy organ-based pop tune that strongly suggested the influence of the Lovin' Spoonful. However, the bulk of the material that appeared on the album was recorded in Los Angeles at Record Plant West, with Artie Ripp producing.

Joel's songwriting skills are plainly evident on *Cold Spring Harbor*. The album's ten tracks demonstrate his developing mastery of musical form. Most are characterized by a fascination with chromaticism as a means for enhancing expressive gesture. The album also features the

influence of many of Joel's favorite artists. In particular, Simon & Garfunkel's *Bridge Over Troubled Water* seems to cast a shadow over the
performances and production style. Coincidentally, many of the same
musicians who played on that album are also present here, as drummer
Rhys Clark points out:

> Well, that album [*Bridge Over Troubled Water*] was still riding high
> on the charts while we were recording with Billy, and I think it did
> have an influence on our approach. Of course, we did have Larry
> Knechtel, who was chosen to play bass guitar, and I must admit that
> Larry seemed a curious choice at the time since he was known main-
> ly as the piano player on "Bridge Over Troubled Water." However,
> he was also an excellent bass player, and his skill on piano seemed to
> inform his bass playing.[26]

Guitarist Don Evans also played on *Cold Spring Harbor* and found
the musical relationships in the studio to be relaxed and productive: "I
particularly remember the spontaneity . . . Billy sang, and we played—
and that was it."[27] However, he also took note of an emerging tension
caused by Artie Ripp's excessive use of studio time: "The '70s hadn't
quite started, but Artie was very much going in that direction, you
know, camping out in the studio forever. The people with the money
weren't ready to let him do that."[28] As the sessions progressed, tempers
were beginning to flare as a result of Ripp's determination to capture
the ideal take. For the young Billy Joel, "It was like pulling teeth. *This
time can you do it with more feeling?* I hated the strings. I didn't want
the session players. The whole thing was completely overproduced."[29]

In all fairness, we should also point out a curious issue related to
Billy Joel's studio performance practice that tended to complicate the
production of *Cold Spring Harbor*. While recording the basic tracks, he
preferred to play the piano and sing at the same time rather than separ-
ately. Artie Ripp described the challenges that this would create in the
studio:

> Because he's singing, you have a piano microphone that's picking up
> his voice, so doing overdubs on that really generally doesn't work.
> You have to hit it as a live performance in the studio, which has its
> good points and its bad points. You can overdub the harmonies, but
> you can't overdub that lead vocal. . . . Ultimately, you have to have
> this musical erection and orgasm that you have to get to, and every-

one else has to hit it at the same time if you're really going to get that magic.[30]

The most glaring problem with regard to Artie Ripp's original production of *Cold Spring Harbor* had to do with the peculiar speed variation audible on the final release. All of the tracks sound noticeably sharp as compared with how they were originally played in the studio during the sessions. According to Artie Ripp, this shift likely occurred during the mastering sessions:

> The machine that I mixed the master to was running slow. The studio second engineer, rather than running a speed test on every single time we were running a session to make sure the machine was running at 15 IPS, he didn't do that. So I don't know whether every single cut or some cuts wound up being recorded on a machine that was running slow, so that when you put it on a machine that ran at normal, proper, spec speed, it had this little speed-up to it.[31]

Given the realities of the recording process, Ripp's account seems quite likely. Long hours in the studio and the resulting stress and fatigue can certainly lead to the kind of mishap he describes here. However, in those days, there was also a common practice of raising the speed of pop recordings by a fraction of a tone in order to make them sound brighter for radio airplay. A vocal also could be recorded with the tape running slightly slower, so that when it was played back at 15 IPS, it would sound brighter.[32]

At this point, it is difficult to determine whether or not this is what happened during the production of *Cold Spring Harbor*. However, given the prevalence of the kind of practices described above, one is led to wonder. Billy Joel is certainly the kind of artist whose pop style would lend itself to this technique. Thus, it does seem possible that an attempt was made to brighten the tracks. However, Artie Ripp himself maintains that this was not the case: "People said that I speeded up the record. I didn't speed up the record. This was almost like Murphy's Law operating, that if anything could go wrong, everything would go wrong."[33]

In combination with other elements related to his contract, the problem with the condition of the final release of *Cold Spring Harbor* created a major rift between Billy Joel and Artie Ripp. After all the hard work he'd put in to prepare for his big break, Joel felt that the final product had somehow been sabotaged. When he first heard the album, he reportedly ripped it from the turntable, ran outside, and threw it as far as he could.[34] In later years, however, he was much more philosophical about the experience as well as the importance of Artie Ripp to his professional career:

> After all the people in the industry who passed on me, Artie Ripp was the guy who wanted me to be his artist. Nobody else heard it, nobody else wanted to sign me, nobody else was making me a deal. Artie made me a deal. He heard something. Was what he heard what I wanted to be as an artist? No. Was it my vision of what the record should be? No. Was it a good deal? No, it was a horrible deal. But he's the guy who got me on the radar screen.[35]

On its initial release, *Cold Spring Harbor* failed to make the desired impact on the charts. It has now come to be regarded as a pleasant but slight offering from a promising young artist still finding his way. The intriguing title was derived from the lyric of the third track, "Everybody Loves You Now." In Billy Joel's hands, a local Long Island hamlet became a youthful paradise in which the singer and his woman can find true and lasting happiness. As the album unfolds, however, this idyllic world is increasingly challenged by the harsh impending realities of young adulthood.

"She's Got a Way"

Cold Spring Harbor begins with a stately and emotionally direct ballad, "She's Got a Way." The song would prove to be an ideal opener, since it served to locate the source of the idyllic world in which the album's story takes place. The lyric describes the seemingly magical power of a woman's love. With a peculiar mixture of wonder and regret, she is described in a semi-mythical fashion driven by the singer's admiration of her abilities. He seems particularly fascinated by the way she shows him new worlds of experience and, in the process, also provides emotional support.

Musically, "She's Got a Way" seems primarily inspired by the Beatles' "For No One" from *Revolver* (1966). However, it also possesses an intriguing hymn-like quality that recalls the title track from the group's final release, *Let It Be* (1970). Essentially, this is a standard variety pop ballad form that every composer has the right to use. The challenge, of course, is to try to find a way to make it unique. Billy Joel succeeds in this regard, primarily through the use of a remarkable series of ascending chords that appear during the concluding cadence of each verse.

There is an intriguing difference between the live and studio versions of "She's Got a Way." During live performance, Joel has used the aforementioned ascending chord sequence to fully end the song on the tonic chord. However, on *Cold Spring Harbor*, he opts to end inconclusively with the first of these chords, an E-flat major seventh. This ending seems to hang in mid-air and point toward the possibility of resolutions to come. In that regard, it seems similar to the curious seventh chord at the end of the Beatles' "Mother Nature's Son," as described by Tim Riley:

> Over a final verse, the brass drops out for Paul to hum over a fine guitar counterpoint (right). As he finishes things off, brass re-enters and plays a flatted seventh on the final chord, mocking the song's literal intentions like a deliberately satirical question mark.[36]

The "satirical question mark" that Tim Riley describes is consistent with the detached irony of *The Beatles* (1968) in that it leaves things decidedly off kilter. Through this subtle yet effective brushstroke in the musical setting, the title of the song effectively changes from "Mother Nature's Son" to "Mother Nature's Son?" In the process, we are reminded that the Beatles could never actually lay claim to the American folk music they are employing here. We also understand that singer/composer Paul McCartney couldn't be the character he is portraying in his performance—it's all part of the game.

In "She's Got a Way," Joel creates a similar rhetorical effect with an ambiguous final chord that generates a sense of unresolved expectation. Instead of completing the previously heard motion to the final tonic (home) chord, the track ends on the expectation of fulfillment. This is a very effective idea for an opening track, since it serves to whet the listener's appetite for what will follow. At the same time, the chord implies doubt as to the sentiments just expressed in the text. Is the singer reading his situation correctly, or is he being swept away by an infatuation that can't possibly last? The rest of *Cold Spring Harbor* will attempt to answer that question.

"Everybody Loves You Now"

"Everybody Loves You Now" is the first break in the idyllic landscape of *Cold Spring Harbor*. Here, Joel explores the affinities between two distinct compositional styles and attempts to blend them together into a viable folk/pop/rock format. The models here are the harmonic and melodic sensibilities of the Beatles combined with the lyrical and structural attitudes of Bob Dylan. Since these artists are known to have influenced and been influenced by one another, this was an astute compositional choice. He sets these distinct elements in an oppositional relationship between the texts of verse and chorus.

The verse of "Everybody Loves You Now" provides a highly critical account of the activities of a former lover. The singer describes her as one who seeks the spotlight at the expense of everyone around her. Consequently, he believes that her recent popularity will inevitably lead to a lonely isolation. As the song progresses, he describes places they have visited and times they shared together, which evidently are no longer important to her. However, in contrast with all the hard feeling and recrimination presented early on, the singer ultimately reveals that he has not given up, and is still waiting anxiously for her to return.

Joel accesses the lyrical approach of Bob Dylan in the litany of deeds that are causing the singer grief. The specific models would seem to be Dylan's 1965 singles, "Positively 4th Street" and "Like a Rolling Stone." Joel also employs a strategy reminiscent of Randy Newman, in that he creates an unreliable first-person narrator. The singer begins by blaming his lost love for all that is wrong with his life, but ultimately reveals that he is waiting for her to reach out to him. Thus, the point of the song is not the critical personal commentary, but rather the simple fact that he is lonely and hurt.

The musical setting for the somewhat venomous lyric is a rollicking pattern on acoustic guitar played by Don Evans, which Billy Joel shadows on acoustic piano. The chord progression bears some similarity to the Beatles' "You Won't See Me," a song that also shares lyrical connections with "Everybody Loves You Now." The Beatles contrast the urgency of their lyric with the cool swagger of mid-'60s pop, whereas Joel's breathless rhythms and agitated harmonies evoke the emotions of his text in a more consistent manner. The listener could almost consider his version to be a continuation of "You Won't See Me," or perhaps even an improvement in terms of dramatic power.

The somewhat slower descending chords of the middle eight create high relief with the rhythmic drive of the verses. Suddenly, in the midst of this descent, a decidedly unstable chord stops the action completely. As a result, the singer is suspended in limbo before falling softly into a plagal (Amen) cadence in minor. This cadence then resolves with the first chord of the return of the opening riff.

"Falling of the Rain"

"Falling of the Rain"[37] is a complex tale that consists of three interconnected vignettes about art and perception. The first concerns a man who spends all of his time painting scenes from nature. Even though he is immersed in the forest that is his subject, his art process necessarily places himself outside the frame of reference. Consequently, he seems curiously oblivious to a natural element that should seem quite evident—the rainfall. This is strongly contrasted by the next vignette in which a young girl lives in the same forest, but is thoroughly immersed in her environment. She dances in celebration of the rain and creatively braids her hair in seeming emulation of natural design.

The third vignette concerns a young man (boy) who appears to be struggling with the pains of an impending maturity. He casts his eyes downward and seems immersed in a melodrama of his own creation. Unlike the girl who dances through the world, he keeps his distance and is determinedly alone and apart. In the final vignette, we learn that the young man was in fact the painter presented in the first vignette, and that his self-imposed isolation has now manifested itself in his art. The young girl has now moved on, suggesting that she was, like nature, always in motion and always on her way to becoming.

The musical setting creates a truly remarkable soundscape that effectively evokes the internal and external worlds of the characters presented in the text. The piano arpeggiations of the introduction mimetically capture the sound of falling rain at a breakneck speed that also connects with the young girl's excited forest dancing. In the first section, this pattern emerges in a lower register solemnly accompanied by bass guitar—the stoicism of the boy/man. In the second section a harpsichord appears, accompanied by very subtle cymbal work. The harpsi-

chord line expands the color of the sound to suggest a connection between rain and snowfall (the passing of time), while the cymbals delightfully evoke the sound of splashing water.

In the contrasting bridge section, a string orchestration echoes ges-
tural elements in the piano part. These melodic lines are fragmentary
and suggest the subtle brushstrokes of an oil painting or watercolor.
Sonically, this creates a tangible image of storm-like weather, thus im-
plying that the listener is standing in the midst of a windy rainstorm.
These qualities continue to flow into the restatement of the introduction and also into the next verse, where it seems that the storm is now
intensifying. The bass drum pattern completes the auditory image as
the low rumblings of thunder before the final chord that seems to
splash outward on the word "rain."

Listening to "Falling of the Rain," one is immediately struck by the
creative work of the various collaborators. Drummer Rhys Clark describes the overall recording process:

> During the early sessions, Larry [Knechtel], Don Evans, and I came
> together with Billy to record the basics with arranger Jimmy Haskell,
> meaning charts, not rehearsals. So, that was an added pressure! But,
> I'm glad we did that because it gave us a chance to develop various
> musical gestures in the arrangements that helped bring out the im-
> agery in Billy's lyrics.[38]

The song's placement on the original LP (as the closer to side one)
suggests that "Falling of the Rain" may have been envisioned as a defin-
ing moment for the entire project. Still, aside from the mastering issues
that were discussed earlier, there are also some noticeable drawbacks in
the final mix. Halfway through the track, the placement of sounds becomes rather static in a manner that tends to upstage the final cadence.
Also, Haskell's orchestration is placed so low in the mix that it seems to
be in danger of disappearing altogether. However, despite its production flaws, "Falling of the Rain" reveals Billy Joel's remarkable ability to
integrate a variety of aural and visual effects within his still-developing
musical style.

"Tomorrow Is Today"

Finally, we have "Tomorrow Is Today," the song that concludes the journey of *Cold Spring Harbor*. The text describes a forlorn state in which the singer has apparently arrived at a personal cul-de-sac. The dreams of his adolescence, once so beautiful and inspired, have morphed into a static existence filled with despair. The lyric is beautifully rendered, but relentless in its portrayal of the seeming apocalypse of young adulthood. In spite of this seeming embrace of hopelessness, there is also a desire to find healing waters that may provide the singer with redemption and renewal. [39]

The musical setting is curiously out of step with the tone of the text. Here, Joel creates a valedictory hymn that suggests transformation and redemption. However, when taken with much of the lyrical content, the listener also wonders if there is an ironic intention at work. Is he cynically marching toward an embrace of absolute despair? Fortunately, this is only a temporary situation that is remedied by the song's eccentric bridge.

As previously noted, "Tomorrow Is Today" establishes a hymn-like quality that lends a solemn tone to the proceedings. The ascending chord progression played by Billy Joel on piano evokes the spirited elegance of J. S. Bach, but he takes the opportunity to extend these chords with subtle elements that suggest the influence of jazz pianist Bill Evans. The most remarkable brushstroke may well be Joel's use of a varied form of the unstable chord heard in the climactic contrasting section of "Everybody Loves You Now." This time, however, the chord does not announce its presence with a full stop. Instead, it glides gracefully past us like water over a pebble. [40]

The bridge section abruptly breaks the somber mood with a series of bold descending chords that suggest the influence of American gospel. While the text explores the possibility of renewal, the music begins to move relentlessly downward. The perilous climb of the earlier sections gives way to the sense that the singer must hit rock bottom before starting over. The music then arrives at a full stop and begins a tentative climb upward toward a restatement of the opening material. In the restatement, there is now an increased energy in the overall performance, suggesting that although the singer may not be completely ready to surrender his cynicism, he's very close.

Following the powerful emotions expressed in "Tomorrow Is To-day," Joel concludes his first album with two interesting tracks. First, there is a piano instrumental titled "Nocturne." As the name suggests, this is a night piece that exists in darkness, but also allows for quiet meditation in the form of dreams. We are then awakened with "Got to Begin Again," a song in the key of G major, which serves to resolve the cadential question that left the listener hanging at the end of "She's Got a Way." It also suggests that the preceding tracks/songs/stories all took place within that resolution. The lyric expresses the singer's willingness to finally let go of the idyllic fantasy world in which he'd been trying to live. He now understands that escape can only be a temporary solution, and that we all must ultimately wake up, face reality, and try again.

2

THE STREETLIFE SERENADER

Despondent over the commercial failure of *Cold Spring Harbor*, Billy Joel resolved to break his contract with Family Productions. He had spent the previous year touring extensively, but it was all for naught. The fledgling company couldn't generate the level of promotion necessary to help the album to find its audience, and Artie Ripp was also running out of funds to support the tour. Thus, it became clear to Billy Joel that *Cold Spring Harbor* was not to be the big breakthrough he had envisioned. It was time to move on.

> I went on tour for six months, I literally lived on the road for six months, and I had a band together and nobody got paid. Cigarette money, you know, and sometimes we'd get meals taken care of, but mostly we paid for our own food. After six months we were going: "Hey! What's going on? Aren't we going to get any money?" I was told: "Oh, it's all promotion!" And I found out there was a lot of money that went by. But after that album I split, after that six-month tour, I just got fed up.[1]

Joel did "split," and in the process, he adopted a very interesting strategy in an effort to change the direction of his career. Returning to the West Coast, he effectively disappeared from the music business. Using the pseudonym "Bill Martin," he performed for six months at a Los Angeles piano bar called the Executive Room. The experience would prove useful in that it allowed him to study the colorful characters and personalities that were regular patrons at the bar. Ultimately, these characters would find their way into his first hit, "Piano Man."[2]

In the meantime, a live radio concert Joel had given the previous year for WMMR radio in Philadelphia was generating some peculiar attention. The broadcast itself had featured a powerful new song of Joel's, "Captain Jack." Following the concert, disc jockey Ed Scialky began receiving requests for the track from listeners who'd heard it during the original broadcast. He played the live recording, and this generated even more listener interest. Soon, "Captain Jack" became the most requested track in the history of WMMR.[3]

The regional success of "Captain Jack" piqued the interest of Columbia Records. The spontaneous nature of the song's appeal suggested to Clive Davis that Joel was a musical force to be reckoned with.[4] In the meantime, Artie Ripp had been attempting to smooth out his relationship with the singer by negotiating a deal for him with Atlantic Records. Billy, however, had his heart set on recording for Columbia. He subsequently signed with the label and returned to the studio to record his second album, *Piano Man* (1973), with veteran L.A. producer Michael Stewart.[5]

ENTER MICHAEL STEWART

One of the benefits of working with Artie Ripp was that it could plug you into the complex network of the music business. Ripp clearly had connections that helped create significant inroads for Billy Joel. Although he was only two years into his solo career, the young artist had already released his first solo album. In the process, he had worked with such studio luminaries as Larry Knechtel, Joe Osborn, and Jimmie Haskell. He had toured as an opening act for a number of first-tier pop and rock artists, and was quickly gaining a reputation as an exciting performer in his own right. Now, he had secured a contract with Columbia Records and would begin to work with a producer named Michael Stewart.

At the time, Michael Stewart was best known for having been a key member of We Five, a folk rock ensemble that scored a hit in 1965 with "You Were on My Mind."[6] His older brother, John Stewart, had been a member of the folk group the Kingston Trio, and also composed "Daydream Believer," which had been a hit for the Monkees in 1967.[7] Following his success with We Five, Michael became known as a creative and empathetic producer who could help new artists develop their potential. This made him an ideal choice to help Billy Joel find his artistic voice in the studio. In the book, *Wounds to Bind: A Memoir of the Folk-Rock Revolution*, author Jerry Burgan describes how their collaboration came about:

> They met because Mike [Stewart] was doing independent work for Family Productions—the company Joel signed with when he got his name back, but before he kissed off L.A. and hooked up with Phil Ramone. In this interlude, Mike produced what would become two landmark albums of the 1970s: *Piano Man* and *Streetlife Serenade*.[8]

Since he'd already had a career of his own, Stewart understood the perks and the pitfalls of pop stardom. He could thus become a suitable mentor for Billy Joel, who was still finding his way as a recording artist. This mentoring process would continue even after the end of their professional relationship, as Jerry Burgan points out: "In later years, when Billy Joel's life got busy and crazy and he couldn't find time to write songs, Mike warned him sternly not to let it happen. . . . It was a subject he knew something about."[9]

PIANO MAN (1973)

Overview

On *Piano Man*, Billy Joel continued to expand and develop his musical palette. As previously noted, *Cold Spring Harbor* consisted largely of self-portraits. Any characters that were presented seemed to work as stand-ins for Billy Joel himself or for his love interest. Here, he begins to shift the focus increasingly toward character studies. He finds his voice by stepping back, and Michael Stewart gives him the creative space to do so.

Stewart's approach in the studio was considerably different from that of Artie Ripp. As discussed in chapter 1, the recording sessions for *Cold Spring Harbor* had been somewhat chaotic. It seems that as Ripp tirelessly searched for a production sound, he would exhaust and frustrate his musicians with an excessive number of takes. This kind of approach can lead to diminishing returns. Since it also requires additional studio time, it can raise the cost of the entire production.

In contrast, Michael Stewart's approach was the model of studio efficiency. In advance of the actual session, Michael Omartian would prepare the arrangements and provide charts for the players.[10] In addition, Stewart opted to use session musicians like Ron Tutt, Wilton Felder, and Dean Parks—all among the best in the business. Thus, there were likely to be fewer mishaps during the recording process. Although the use of session players would later become a sticking point for Joel, the example set by their virtuosity seems to have enhanced the level of his own vocal and piano performances.

"Piano Man"

Anyone who has ever played music in a bar or restaurant understands the way in which that gig tends to carry with it a peculiar mixture of detachment and control. The musician quickly realizes that the customers usually aren't paying close attention. They certainly hear what is being played, but they're generally more preoccupied with their personal lives, their private conversations, or the meals they've come to enjoy. While this kind of invisibility can initially be rather frustrating for a musician, it also allows for a subtle control of the room's ambience. Through careful attention to the overall mood, the musician can subliminally soothe and please the patrons with an appropriate choice of song or patter.

As previously noted, in an effort to break his contract with Artie Ripp and Family Productions, Billy Joel took up an anonymous residency at an L.A. club, the Executive Room. He initially found the job tedious due to the lack of the appreciation he would feel during the gig. However, the lyric to "Piano Man" suggests that Joel soon got past his initial frustration and began to consider the patrons as possible subjects for his next batch of songs. Joel took note of the details each tended to reveal about his or her own life experience. He then sketched his verses around the patrons' dreams and aspirations, which seemed, for the most part, to have gone unfulfilled.

First, there is the old man who is preoccupied with his gin and tonic and the memories of his youth. Next comes John the bartender, a co-worker who provides the singer with drinks while dreaming of movie stardom. John also serves drinks to a real estate agent and bachelor named Paul, who discusses his ambition to write novels with a young sailor named Davy. Finally, we have a waitress who likes to talk politics with the businessmen getting drunk at the bar. These businessmen seem more interested in her appearance than her political ideas.

As sketched by Billy Joel, the lives of these characters seem to access the style of the painter Edward Hopper, who was known for his ability to create uncannily authentic renderings of human life and culture. In a similar manner, Joel's characters are presented in vivid musical portraits that serve to foreground their basic humanity. Together, they become part of a virtual gallery that seems to portend the world of *The Stranger* (1977). There, Billy Joel will explore the ways in which his various characters escape the restrictions of their humdrum lives. Here, it is the "Piano Man" himself that must get away before it is too late.

The musical setting for "Piano Man" draws from a variety of sources. The circular arpeggiations of the piano introduction, along with the simple harmonica line, suggests the influence of Dylan's "Just Like a Woman" and "Desolation Row." In addition, the song's reliance on a descending bass line recalls the Jerry Jeff Walker song "Mr. Bojangles," famously covered by the Nitty Gritty Dirt Band in 1970. There also seems to be a subtle Celtic influence in the arrangement that suggests the troubadour. As he had done in the past, Joel once again transposes acoustic guitar patterns to the piano to help enhance this effect.

Over time, the image of the "Piano Man" became burdensome for Joel. It tended to pigeonhole him in a way that undercut the eclectic variety that he sought in his writing. In spite of this, the song itself seems to be a turning point in his development as an artist. It reaches beyond the autobiographical focus of *Cold Spring Harbor* in order to enhance the scope and subject matter of his subsequent works. In a sense, "Piano Man" acts as a prism, which the composer himself passes through in order to *become* Billy Joel.

"The Ballad of Billy the Kid"

Just as he was beginning to move away from the first-person narratives that had characterized *Cold Spring Harbor*, Billy Joel offered listeners a song that played with their expectations for biographical elements in his work. Following what seems to be an accurate account of the life and legend of William H. Bonney (Billy the Kid), the final verse/coda suggests that the author himself has entered the text to become a Borgesian latter-day double for the main character. However, even this narrative conceit is suspect. The liner notes from the 1981 album *Songs in the Attic* reveal that the boy from Oyster Bay, Long Island, is not Billy Joel. Rather, he is a bartender that Joel knew from his glory days back on Long Island.[11]

Although "The Ballad of Billy the Kid" definitely sounds like it is providing an accurate account of the life of the main character, the lyric was a fabrication from start to finish, and had little to do with the actual William H. Bonney. As Joel himself points out, the song "was an experiment with an impressionist type of lyric. It was historically totally inaccurate . . . it wasn't supposed to be listened to as a story."[12] Despite the creative subterfuge, the lyric itself is remarkably effective. Joel's images are so vivid that they take on a power that reaches for the cinematic. In particular, the verse that describes the death of Billy the Kid is at once awe inspiring in its "historical" sweep, and deeply moving in its evocation of human mortality.

The vivid imagery and clever narrative strategy of "The Ballad of Billy the Kid" are enhanced by the song's remarkable orchestration. Here, Jimmie Haskell (with some help from Joel) conjures up a Western soundscape that convincingly portrays the expansive vistas of the American frontier.[13] As music scholar Walter Everett points out, the instrumentation simultaneously references "classical" music and the film scoring techniques of the Hollywood Western:

> The song's instrumental break (piano and horns with countermelody in strings) also has the quality of—but no quotes from—sections of Copland's "Rodeo" and (naturally) "Billy the Kid"; the composer once characterized his song . . . as "Elmer Bernstein shot in hot blood by the infamous Newman brothers, Alfred and Lionel, avenging the murder of Aaron Copland."[14]

In 2008, producer Phil Ramone pointed out that the only thing Billy Joel had yet to do was score a film. It seems that with "The Ballad of Billy the Kid," he achieved that goal in miniature.[15] The orchestral gestures derived from cinema are sweeping and assured. Combined with his choice of subject matter, these help create a uniquely original sound recording. With "The Ballad of Billy the Kid," Joel had pushed song form into the realm of the symphonic and, in the process, began to explore the language of cinema as a means for expanding the scope of his recorded works.

"Stop in Nevada"

On "Stop in Nevada," Billy Joel continued to explore and develop a character-driven approach to songwriting. The lyric concerns a young woman who has left behind a seemingly tranquil existence as wife and mother in order to find a new life in California. She hopes that this new life may provide the kind of personal fulfillment she was unable to achieve at home. Interestingly, the tale is told in broad strokes, allowing the listener to wonder about what we're not being told about this woman's life. Further, we never learn what happens to her in California.

In this early part of his career, Billy Joel was categorized as a singer-songwriter on the order of James Taylor, Harry Chapin, or Gordon Lightfoot. However, guitarist Don Evans challenges this view by pointing out that Joel "tends to paint pictures of people and events—kind of like mini-movies. To me, that's closer to the way Billy worked."[16] Joel's nonlinear narratives differ from those of the singer-songwriter in that they are less concerned with resolution than they are with suggesting the cultural environments of his characters. This quality contrasts well with the directed tonal motion of his musical settings.

Like "Traveling Prayer" from *Piano Man*, and "Turn Around" from *Cold Spring Harbor*, this modestly effective song is another attempt by Joel to incorporate country and western elements into his sound. The tasteful arrangement by Michael Omartian features superb pedal steel work by Tom Whitehorse, and in the process seems to reference "The Most Beautiful Girl in the World," recorded by Charlie Rich in early 1973. Adding to the country and western effect are Joel's subtle piano riffs that suggest the influence of country music legend Floyd Cramer.

All of this is topped off by a rocking orchestration that lends a passionate gospel-like intensity to the proceedings.

"Captain Jack"

The grand finale of *Piano Man* is "Captain Jack," a song that perfects the epic narrative style that had interested Joel as far back as "Hotel St. George" (1969). Several tracks on the *Piano Man* album have prepared listeners for this approach: "The Ballad of Billy the Kid" does so as a kind of postmodern parody that tentatively aspires toward mixed media through its musical references to classic cinema. "Stop in Nevada" comes much closer to "Captain Jack" in terms of musical form with alternating sections (verse and chorus) that battle it out as the song proceeds. However, whereas the contrasting sections of "Stop in Nevada" can seem a bit too evenly balanced, "Captain Jack" allows the tension to build with an extended verse that evokes a kind of cultural stasis before the climactic explosions of the chorus.

As on "Piano Man," the listener can once again detect the influence of Bob Dylan, but Joel's imagery here is truly his own. In fact, the world of the song seems to be one that he knows quite well. There is an intriguing obscurity about the track that lingers more than forty years on. Who exactly is this Captain Jack character that so piqued the interest of WMMR listeners in 1972? According to Joel, the character is as an amalgam of a variety of cultural types that inhabited the vast suburban wasteland of his youth:

> Well, the character in "Captain Jack" was a composite of different kinds of people. I was just sitting around one day looking out of the window wondering what I was going to write about, and kinda wrote about what was going on outside. I mean, Long Island is a suburb and it was about a suburban type of character. There's a lot of frustration living in the suburbs—you don't have an identity as you would if you came from the city or the country, there's city music and there's country music, but there's really no suburban music, you kinda copy the city. You have both influences pulling on you.[17]

The song's lyric addresses another postadolescent male who just can't seem to get his life on track. In keeping with Joel's description, this man-child is pulled in a variety of different directions regarding style and fashion, but nothing seems to stick. Although he is at an age when a man tends to be in demand socially, the center of his life is revealed as being hollow and obscure. Like many twenty-somethings who lack direction, he attempts to fill the emptiness with artificial highs that can only provide a temporary relief from the tedium. The local supplier of this pseudo-satisfaction is none other than a pseudo-hipster named "Captain Jack."

As compared with other tracks from *Piano Man*, the musical arrangement of "Captain Jack" is remarkably expansive, and a considerable amount of credit for this should go to drummer Rhys Clark. At this point, Clark had been working with Joel for several years, both in concert and in the studio. Thus, it seems significant that his sole performance contribution to the sessions for *Piano Man* stands in stark contrast to the more hurried style of Michael Stewart's go-to session players. From the majestic cymbal rollout of the church organ introduction to the exhilarating transitions between verse and chorus, Clark's drum work helps paint the sprawling cultural landscape of the main character in broad and vivid strokes.

INTERLUDE: BILLY JOEL AND ELTON JOHN

In October 1973, one month before the appearance of *Piano Man*, Elton John unleashed his mammoth double LP *Goodbye Yellow Brick Road*.[18] This landmark pop recording would dominate radio airplay into the following year and would generally come to be regarded as the artist's masterpiece. The album demonstrates that by late 1973, Elton and his collaborators had mastered the nostalgic approach to pop that had been a key feature of his previous albums, *Don't Shoot Me I'm Only the Piano Player* (1973) and *Honky Chateau* (1972).

Elton John clearly had a marked influence on Billy Joel who, at this point, was still finding his way as a solo artist. It's been suggested that *Tumbleweed Connection* (1970), Elton's concept album about the American West, was an influence on the production strategy of *Piano Man*. In an interview for this study, guitarist Don Evans concurred with this idea: "That album might have inspired a few of the tracks because we had definitely heard it—Elton's first album too, the one with the big orchestrations. . . . Everything he [Joel] heard that was orchestral, he kind of wanted to do." Evans also commented on Joel's resistance to categorization by style:

> After *Piano Man*, there was a tendency to lump him in there with people like Jim Croce or Harry Chapin. In other words, he was being tagged as a storytelling songwriter, and he kind of resisted that. He didn't want to be thought of in that way. He also didn't want to be the next Elton John. I mean, their names were right next to each other in the record rack. He could do a good Elton John impression, but was always quick to point out the differences.[19]

Despite the acknowledged similarities, the approaches of Elton John and Billy Joel are quite distinct.[20] Elton John's piano work is distinguished by its unpredictable approach to rhythm. Songs such as "Amoreena" from *Tumbleweed Connection* (1970), and "Susie (Dramas)" from *Honky Chateau* (1972), exhibit a syncopation that suggests the influence of blues and gospel via the music of Leon Russell. By contrast, Billy Joel's piano style tends to lean more toward regularity in its adherence to the sixteenth-note patterns associated with classical piano technique, such as in "Root Beer Rag" from *Streetlife Serenade* (1974), and "Falling of the Rain" from *Cold Spring Harbor* (1971).

In an obscure filmed interview from the mid-1970s, Billy Joel directly addressed these differences:

> Elton really broke the piano pop barrier and he became the definitive piano rock artist. And anyone who became known after him was compared to Elton John. I don't play the same way he does. Elton's style is very rhythmic, you know. Or, like, Leon Russell is another guy I used to get comparisons to. And he's more like gospel, you know. And my style is probably—it's more five-finger, more movement stuff.[21]

Another factor to consider regarding the differences between Billy Joel and Elton John concerns how each artist approaches jazz. Joel had developed his skills in this genre by studying with pianist/composer Lennie Tristano, and this influence soon found its way into his songwriting through the use of complex chord voicings.[22] In the next few years, this influence would become even more pronounced on tracks like "New York State of Mind" and "James" from *Turnstiles* (1976), as well as "Rosalinda's Eyes" and "Zanzibar" from *52nd Street* (1978). In the final analysis, Joel's integration of jazz-derived elements into pop rock would be regarded as one of his most important contributions.

In contrast, Elton John seemed to understand jazz from a distance. Despite his acknowledged brilliance with country, blues, and gospel, he was seemingly unable to incorporate American jazz into his own compositions. John's first album, *Empty Sky* (1969), does feature an instrumental called "Hay Chewed" that attempts to reach for a jazz style. However, it quickly becomes a rollicking jam that might best be described as "jazzy." The listener should take note of the very convincing piano solo featured in the otherwise R&B flavored "Bennie and the Jets," but following that, he seemed to abandon the idea completely.

The release of *Goodbye Yellow Brick Road* would mark the peak of Elton John's fame and influence. Even though he would continue to have great success with *Caribou* (1974) and *Captain Fantastic and the Brown Dirt Cowboy* (1975), the consensus that had come to characterize his early work had largely begun to dissolve. He still had a loyal fan base, but no longer seemed to be channeling the cultural mood the way he had been in the early 1970s. This effectively opened up a space for Billy Joel to develop his own ideas regarding music composition and album production. He would do just that with his next release, *Streetlife Serenade* (1974).

STREETLIFE SERENADE

Overview

The lack of commercial impact and limited distribution of *Cold Spring Harbor* meant that *Piano Man* (1973) would ultimately be perceived as Joel's debut album. Since it had been a commercial success, Columbia executives were pressing him for a follow-up. So, while touring in early 1974, he labored to write another song cycle that could be recorded and ready for release by the following autumn. He described the experience of dealing with this pressure: "You spend your youth building up material . . . that tells your story, and then, in the middle of abruptly finding success and crashing in Holiday Inns . . . you have a couple months to write ten or twelve heartfelt new songs."[23]

Billy Joel went back into the studio with Michael Stewart to record *Streetlife Serenade*. The production strategy for the new album was essentially the same as for *Piano Man*, with one notable exception—arranger Michael Omartian was not included. Instead, the album's liner notes credited Michael Stewart and Billy Joel as arrangers for the sessions. In a 1975 interview with Andy Childs for *Zigzag* magazine, Joel explained the reasons for this change:

> I wanted to make this album a lot simpler. I wanted to keep it within the framework of a streetlife kind of sound. I didn't want a big orchestral happening. It was kind of a concept album, not so much a concept from beginning to end, it's just the overall production and the feeling of the material—a streetlife concept.[24]

The move away from complex arrangements and toward simplicity that Billy Joel describes here had an interesting effect on the overall sound of *Streetlife Serenade*.

The instrumentation that had characterized *Piano Man* had a monochromatic quality that was well suited to the album's quasi-Western themes. The resulting effect suggested that the album was a collection of sketches in black and white. With *Streetlife Serenade*, Joel would simplify the arrangements in order to focus more on musical color or timbre, which *Grove Music Online* defines as "the tonal quality of a sound; a clarinet and an oboe sounding the same note at the same loudness are said to produce different timbres."[25] This also connected with some of the most progressive ideas in twentieth-century music:

> In the 20th century the temporal differences between colours and notes, or music and painting, were no longer seen as irreconcilable. . . . As early as Schoenberg's Farben, from *Five Orchestral Pieces* (1909), the two themes are reduced to their smallest possible extent both in number of notes and in range; the melodic function is obliterated, and only tonal colour remains. The composition may be seen as an attempt to transfer to music the wide variety of shades of a single colour found in painting, extending the opportunities open to music by the attempt to compose in colour.[26]

In this way, the transition from *Piano Man* to *Streetlife Serenade* can be considered as a movement into color. As an aid in this process, Joel made full use of his newly acquired Moog synthesizer.

Developed in early 1964 by Robert A. Moog, this exotic instrument had initially been used as a novelty effect on a variety of popular record-ings.[27] This kind of approach is echoed on *Streetlife Serenade* with the tracks "The Great Suburban Showdown" and "Root Beer Rag." In the early 1970s, the Moog's symphonic potential had been explored exten-sively by bands like Yes, Genesis, and Emerson, Lake & Palmer. Billy Joel builds on this idea with the seeming orchestral pads that are used to enhance the textures of "Roberta" and "The Mexican Connection." The album's sole single release, "The Entertainer," embodies both of these approaches through its exotic introductory riff and its extraordi-narily subtle blend of synthesizer and steel guitar throughout.

"Streetlife Serenader"

The opening and near-title track of *Streetlife Serenade* is a majestic ballad that seeks to paint a cultural landscape for the character sketches to follow. The title refers to the neighborhood street singing that Billy Joel engaged in during his youth. Composer Ira Newborn describes how he would sing harmony with Joel in various locations that were selected for their special reverberant qualities:

> Yes, well that's a standard doo-wop thing . . . looking for anyplace with reverb such as subways, alleyways, or store entrances where there was glass on either side, and it was good. . . . At the time, we used to sing with three or four different people. The most we ever had at one time was five . . . I'll never forget that. And it was the first time that I ever had a real feeling of MUSIC with a bunch of other people. And it was like, "Wow, this is unbelievable."[28]

The lyric never explicitly describes the activity of street singing. Rather, it uses broad brushstrokes that reveal the cultural origins of the main character. We learn that he is a baby boomer born just after World War II, and thus has high expectations for the newly liberated world into which he has emerged. He also has musical talent but pre-fers to remain an amateur, singing with his friends for his own enjoy-ment. Nevertheless, it is implied that in this practice, the streetlife serenader performs a vital social function in reporting on the cultural life that is happening all around him.

The musical setting is particularly interesting in that it seeks to build on the rich and expansive soundscapes of "Captain Jack." Joel's piano introduction mimes the whole tone structure of that song before stretching upward an additional whole step for the verse. Curiously, there are no true choruses here. Instead, we get a recurring instrumental interlude on piano that is punctuated by martial-sounding rolls, played on the snare drum by Ron Tutt. Together, these elements suggest an uneasy truce between polite society and the inherent savagery of human conflict. A second interlude serves as the transition into a soaring guitar solo, played by Al Hertzberg.

Billy Joel's impressionistic piano work suggests the influence of composer Claude Debussy, and leads the ensemble into a rich fabric of musical color. This contrasts well with the lyric's portrayal of a pallid postwar life that serves as the raw material for the artistry of the main character. Still, despite the fact that the track constitutes a clear departure for Joel in terms of sound, the listener gets the sense that it is somehow incomplete. In the liner notes for *Songs in the Attic* (1981), which featured a live version of "Streetlife Serenader," he describes the song as "one of the most emotionally satisfying compositions I've ever attempted . . . I gave Debussy a good beating. He won."[29]

"Roberta"

The first side of *Streetlife Serenade* closes with "Roberta," a track that seems to be the album's only genuine love song. On the surface, the lyric is an earnest, yet somewhat naïve paean to a young woman who is clearly unavailable. However, when we look more closely at the text, we begin to realize that this is actually a love song to a prostitute. The lyric makes several coy allusions to the world's oldest profession, as the singer gallantly takes the blame for not being able to take care of Roberta due to his lack of finances. He also implies that he knows that he is not the only one, but doesn't care, because he wants her all the same.

From *Don Quixote* to *Pretty Woman*, the theme of falling for a prostitute has a long and fruitful tradition. "Roberta" is itself a part of that tradition and predates Sting's "Roxanne" by over three years. Joel's twist on this theme is that we're not really sure about the motives of the main character. Does he really love Roberta, or is this simply a clever game that he is playing in order to temporarily gain her affection? This curious ambiguity helps knock the song off kilter and, in the process, works to hold the listener's interest.

The music of "Roberta" opens with an introduction borrowed from "I Am . . . I Said" by Neil Diamond. Billy Joel's version is modified, however, so that the riff is played in reverse. The melody in the verse dances in playful syncopation with the underlying pulse. In this way, Joel seems to reference Elton John's use of unusual accents that appear within the context of his piano playing. In "Roberta," however, they are not just a feature of the piano accompaniment; they are also an integral part of the song's musical structure.

The setting of "Roberta" also features an instrumental passage/interlude that works in similar fashion to the ones in "Streetlife Serenader." The interlude featured here occurs right after the contrasting bridge section and then again as a kind of coda/fadeout. It is an interesting collation of the verse chords with new motivic material, but its placement has a strange asymmetrical effect on the form of the song. Specifically, it is immediately followed by a piano iteration of the melody of the verse and this seems, in context, to be a needless repetition. Nevertheless, the presence of these interludes suggests that the actual focus of *Streetlife Serenade* arguably rests more on them than on the songs in which they are featured.

The Instrumentals

The album template of the 1970s singer-songwriter did not typically allow for the inclusion of instrumentals. One may be acceptable, but *Streetlife Serenade* includes two: "Root Beer Rag" and "The Mexican Connection." Moreover, instrumental interludes are featured on "Streetlife Serenader" and "Roberta," and there is an extended instrumental coda on "The Great Suburban Showdown." We've already noted that Billy Joel did not have enough songs for this project due to a lack of time between albums. It is interesting, however, that he seems to have viewed these instrumentals as an opportunity to continue to develop his compositional technique.

"Root Beer Rag" is a bravura piece for piano that accesses ragtime by way of vaudeville. Within this framework there are several eclectic features, such as an impressive chordal transition that suggests the influence of a Bach chorale, and a minor key passage that appears only once but manages to add an effective measure of pathos to the proceedings. At times, the track borders on country and western, suggesting a subtle connection between that genre and the music of Scott Joplin. In terms of musical color, "Root Beer Rag" employs the Moog synthesizer, which is used here for a comic effect perfectly appropriate to the ragtime style.

"The Mexican Connection" revisits the sounds that Billy Joel last explored on "Stop in Nevada" and "The Ballad of Billy the Kid." This time, however, we also get a Mexican flavor in keeping with the title of the track. The sound and mood seem to evoke the vast, sweeping landscapes of the American Southwest and northern Mexico. There is also another reference to film composer Elmer Bernstein, as Joel employs riffs and rhythms similar to those last heard on "The Ballad of Billy the Kid." Also, as he had done on "Root Beer Rag," Joel adds baroque elements to "The Mexican Connection" with a keyboard passage that seems to emulate the texture and technique of a two-part invention by J. S. Bach.

The eclectic qualities of these two tracks lend credence to the notion that Billy Joel is a kind of alchemist who blends different musical elements together according to their underlying affinities. If the listener chooses to regard them as mere filler, he or she is free to do so. However, careful listening reveals that in each case, Joel is taking the opportunity to continue to develop as a composer, and as an artist.

"The Entertainer"

Earlier, we noted that arranger Michael Omartian was not listed as a participant on the sessions for *Streetlife Serenade* as he had been for *Piano Man*. Another change was the inclusion of Don Evans, who had played guitar on *Cold Spring Harbor* and was now touring with Billy Joel in that capacity. On *Streetlife Serenade*, Evans plays acoustic rhythm guitar on "The Entertainer," a spirited folk rocker that recalls the energetic and equally cynical "Everybody Loves You Now." Actually, it was Evans who created the driving acoustic guitar parts on both tracks:

> I had been doing "Everybody Loves You Now" on the road all that time, which has a similar kind of drive to it. I always had that Richie

Havens kind of thing . . . there are versions of "The Entertainer" that were made before we officially recorded it. And on those versions, Billy doesn't play at all until the end. Then, Michael came in and completely changed it. He made it more of a piano record . . . the rhythm guitar part did survive, though.[30]

Streetlife Serenade was Joel's most extensive foray into the country and western genre, and "The Entertainer" is arguably his most successful integration of that style. The song's musical setting hearkens back to "Travelin' Prayer" from *Piano Man*, and the lyric offers a cynical account of the life of a performer working in the music business of the 1970s. It describes Joel's frustration in having to compromise his art in order to deal with the realities of the marketplace, as Joel points out: "'The Entertainer' came partly out of the experience of seeing 'Piano Man' downsized from the original six-minute album cut to a three-minute single . . . I don't suppose that little aside did me that much good with the Columbia brass."[31]

"The Entertainer" unfolds with an arrangement that builds the instrumentation, verse by verse, in order to gradually thicken the overall texture. The skillful mixing that is evident on the track creates color through the careful blend of Moog synthesizer with the pedal steel guitar. Also, the entrance of the piano at 1:58 is one of the most thrilling moments on the entire album. This is when the rowdy setting is complete, and the listener would not be surprised to hear gunshots ringing out, suggesting a shootout in the Old West.

As in "The Ballad of Billy the Kid," the main character has the free spirit of the outlaw and the musical setting enhances this perception. In both the arrangement and the production, Billy Joel and Michael Stewart seem to have decided to set the song in a Western saloon. Acoustic guitars, banjos, and a honky-tonk piano all share the stage along with an anachronistic Moog synthesizer that is obscured behind pedal steel guitar. The anger and frustration that Joel expresses in the lyric lends itself to the lawless behavior often featured in old Westerns. As we've seen on *Piano Man*, and will see again on *The Stranger*, cinematic references will play an increasing role in the aesthetics of Billy Joel's music.

3

I'VE LOVED THESE DAYS

Having spent the better part of the early 1970s trying to find his way in L.A., Billy Joel decided it was time to return to New York and reconnect with his roots. Far from being a surrender, we can rightly regard all the hard work on *Cold Spring Harbor, Piano Man*, and *Streetlife Serenade* as a period of apprenticeship in which the young artist fully entered the big leagues of popular music. Working on those albums, Joel collaborated with accomplished record makers like Michael Stewart, Michael Omartian, and Jimmie Haskell. He also raised the level of his musicianship by recording with the top studio musicians of the day. Moreover, this apprenticeship had allowed him to develop the ability to write entire albums on his own, no easy task in the wake of the Beatles, who set an extraordinarily high standard for their contemporaries, and for themselves.

The Beatles were unique in that they featured three composers in the same band. Two of those composers, John Lennon and Paul McCartney, were world class, while the third, George Harrison, was a promising apprentice. Assuming that John Lennon and Paul McCartney each wrote six to ten songs for a recording project, and George Harrison wrote three, it's clear that there would not be enough space on one fourteen-song album to include all of the material. Thus, an editing process emerged whereby the best songs from each composer would be selected for inclusion on a given album. In addition, the Beatles and producer George Martin would edit individual songs and sequences before they ever reached the public ear. This unique collaboration had a challenging, and ultimately withering, effect on the competition.

In the early 1960s, Brian Wilson demonstrated his prodigious talents by writing and producing hit recordings for the Beach Boys. At that time, there was less of an emphasis on albums as complete statements, so he tended to focus his energies on 45 rpm singles. Soon, Wilson began competing with the Beatles' progressively sophisticated song cycles. Their work inspired the Beach Boys' *Pet Sounds* (1966), the 45 rpm single "Good Vibrations," (1966), and the ill-fated *Smile* album (1967). Ultimately, in his ongoing struggle to compete with the Beatles' creative juggernaut, Brian Wilson experienced a professional and personal collapse and only worked sporadically for the next few decades.[1]

Paul Simon was another contemporary of the Beatles who attempted to match their songwriting standard within the context of Simon & Garfunkel. The duo only released five original albums: *Wednesday Morning, 3 A.M.* (1964); *Sounds of Silence* (1966); *Parsley, Sage, Rosemary and Thyme* (1966); *Bookends* (1968); and *Bridge Over Troubled Water* (1970), and also contributed prerecorded material for the film *The Graduate* (1968). In order to meet the Beatles' standard, Simon got into the habit of recycling songs from one project to another. By 1968, Simon's most famous song, "The Sound of Silence," managed to appear in various forms on four different albums![2]

By the early 1970s, singer-songwriters were expected to fill entire albums with their own material on a regular basis. The Beatles themselves had to cope with this new standard during their solo careers. After the breakup, John Lennon started off strong with *Plastic Ono Band* (1970) and *Imagine* (1972). Soon, however, he seemed to lose interest in the process and by 1975, had retired from the music business entirely to focus on home and family life. George Harrison's epic three-disc collection, *All Things Must Pass* (1970), collated the material that did not survive the Beatles' editing process along with some freshly written songs. His subsequent albums maintained a very high level of musicianship and contained the occasional hit single. However, like Lennon, he also seemed to wither from the creative grind associated with popular music.

Generally the most prolific Beatle, Paul McCartney seemed to fare the best in this new environment. He seemed to enjoy the creative challenge of producing new product in a timely manner. His first solo album, *McCartney* (1970), was short on complete songs, due primarily to the fact that he had been writing the majority of original material for the late-period (1967–1970) Beatles albums. However, he soon regained his stride and went on to release some of the most successful albums of the 1970s.

So this was the nature of the competition that Billy Joel had to face in the early 1970s. In that light, the assertion that he can be regarded as a one-man version of the Beatles is not so fanciful. Arguably, the only other real contender for such a title was Elton John. However, Elton had a collaborator in lyricist Bernie Taupin, with whom he'd been writing for two years prior to the release of his first album, *Empty Sky*, in 1969.[3] By contrast, Joel worked by himself and tended to only write as the need arose, creating entire albums as song cycles. Producer Michael Stewart had nurtured Joel through the rigors of this process. In the book, *Wounds to Bind: A Memoir of the Folk-Rock Revolution*, authors Jerry Burgan and Alan Rifkin recount Stewart's experiences working with Billy Joel:

> Joel had done nothing to speak of at the dawn of the '70s. He'd been working in a hotel piano bar in Universal City under the name "Bill Martin," waiting out his contract to a record company that didn't know what to do with him. But Mike [Stewart] did. Joel expressed musical ideas on the fly; and Mike saw at once how to fill the form with musicians and arrangements. Joel later said Mike was the first person to understand what he was all about and succeed in recording it.[4]

Following an attempt by Stewart to record new Billy Joel material at the Great American Music Hall in San Francisco, the two went their separate ways.[5] In later years, Billy himself would readily acknowledge the tremendous support and encouragement he had received from Michael Stewart, but at the time, he was also feeling pressure from his touring band regarding studio time: "I got along good with Michael Stewart. . . .The only time we ran into a problem was when . . . I had a band together that had been on the road for two years and he didn't want me to use them on the recordings."[6]

The new Billy Joel Band would soon come together around the talents of Liberty DeVitto on drums, Doug Stegmeyer on electric bass, Russell Javors on guitar, and Joel himself on piano and keyboards. Ri-

chie Cannata had also been recruited to handle reeds and the occasional keyboard when necessary. Although the process was gradual, this new
band was basically an assimilation of Topper, a group of Long Island
musicians that had formed around the songwriting talents of Russell
Javors.[7]

At around this time, Billy Joel became affiliated with Caribou Management and was being urged to record at the Caribou Ranch with
producer James William Guercio. Elton John had recently recorded
there, and Guercio had great success producing groups like Chicago
and Blood, Sweat & Tears. It seemed like a match made in heaven but
for one glaring problem: Guercio's initial production idea was for Joel to
use Elton John's backing band on the sessions. A series of recordings
were completed, but Joel felt that the sound was too much like Elton's.
Thus, he fired Guercio, left Caribou Management, and asked his wife
Elizabeth to become his manager.[8]

ENTER GEORGE MARTIN?

Billy Joel had now arrived at another turning point. He'd already ended
his working relationships with both Michael Stewart and James William
Guercio. So, the question remained: Who was going to produce his next
album? With poetic flourish, an opportunity emerged that seemed to
validate his status in the industry as well as his own fascination with the
music of the Beatles. In *Billy Joel: The Definitive Biography*, Joel describes what almost happened:

> George Martin was looked on by the music industry as the state-of-
> the-art producer, the Beatles' guy. If you could get George Martin,
> then you must be pretty damn good. He was interested, but when we
> had a conversation, he said, "I've seen you play, I like your stuff. I
> don't like your band. I want you to work with the studio musicians."
> It was a crucial moment because here I had the opportunity to work
> with George Martin, a producer of the band I admired most in the
> world, the Beatles, and he didn't want to work with my band. I said,
> "What do I do?"[9]

Evidently, a compromise could not be reached, so Joel decided to
produce his next album himself. He certainly did a good job, but take a

moment to consider what might have been. Within the Beatles, Martin was the link to the musical traditions of the past. He had been educated at London's Guildhall School of Music and was a brilliant orchestrator and conductor.[10] In addition, Martin seems to have coached the individual members of the Beatles through the rigors of record production. Every member of that band emerged as a producer.

By working with George Martin, Billy Joel would have had an opportunity to further explore not just the nuts and bolts of orchestration, but also the nuances of instrumental color. Joel already had some experience with this process during the preproduction for his first two albums, as he himself points out: "Jimmie Haskell wrote it ["The Ballad of Billy The Kid"] and conducted the string section, but I told him what I wanted. I worked pretty closely with the arrangements on the Cold Spring [Harbor] album."[11] The Beatles had worked closely with Martin on a variety of orchestrations, but Billy Joel had the advantage of actually being able to read music. With further tutelage, he could have absorbed these principles into his own creative process and then applied them to record production. As a mentor, George Martin could have taught him all this and more, but alas, it was not to be.

TURNSTILES (1976)

Overview

Despite turmoil surrounding its creation, *Turnstiles* was a major achievement for Billy Joel. In retrospect, the album constitutes the moment at which he began to move past the inspired innocence of his earlier songs toward a more confident, mature style. The album's production leans toward postmodern homage and, in the process, creates another gallery of short forms on the order of *Piano Man*. Now, however, he was finding interesting ways to extend and vary his musical ideas. From the Phil Spector swagger of "Say Goodbye to Hollywood" to the laid-back Ray Charles sway of "New York State of Mind," the album blends Joel's influences with humor and considerable charm.

The piano as music box introduction and coda to "Miami 2017 (I've Seen the Lights Go Out on Broadway)" seems to meld the haunting piano riff from Mike Oldfield's "Tubular Bells" (1973), with the circular chord progression of the Beatles' "Dear Prudence." Soon, however, the track morphs into a spirited rocker somewhere between Meat Loaf and the E Street Band. "All You Want to Do Is Dance" appropriately and effectively fuses the melodicism of Paul McCartney with the Jamaican grooves of Bob Marley. Finally, "I've Loved These Days" remains one of Joel's most neglected tracks, and sits very comfortably between the balladry of Elton John and the late-period Beatles.

The stylistic variety of *Turnstiles* also showcases Joel's abilities as a mimic without ever letting them get the best of him. Rhys Clark commented on this talent in connection with Billy Joel's early concert tours:

> When we first started playing together, we played in Los Angeles at the Troubadour club. During an interlude, Billy started playing a blues and making up a lyric. In the course of that improvisation he mimicked the voices of a whole bunch of people like Johnny Cash, Joe Cocker, and even old vaudevillian actors like George Jessel.[12]

Guitarist Don Evans concurs: "He could do James Taylor, Leon Russell, Elton John, etc. Every once in a while I hear a bootleg where he's really doing this stuff. . . . He could capture the essence of McCartney and a lot of other people as well."[13]

It's interesting to consider how Joel's live audiences have responded to his talent for mimicry. Rather than regarding it as being inauthentic, they enthusiastically cheer him on. We may wonder if, when mimicking other performers, Billy Joel is actually miming his audience. After a few drinks, most people can be coaxed into singing along with their favorite records. In the process, they would likely try to sound or act like Mick Jagger, Ray Charles, or any of a number of other artists. Thus, Billy Joel's mimetic talent may well be accessing the rock genre's tendency to allow the singer to function as a stand-in for the audience.

Finally, *Turnstiles* is the first Billy Joel release that foregrounds his fascination with American jazz. As asserted in the preface of this book, Billy Joel was the mid-70s man of the moment—born at the right time, with the right set of musical skills. As such, he was well suited to engage with the emergence of a more sophisticated form of pop music. As previously noted, Joel was actually tutored by one of the great jazz musicians of the postwar era. In an interview with pianist Judy Carmichael, Joel describes how, as a teenager, he came to study with pianist and arranger Lennie Tristano:

I took some lessons from Lennie Tristano . . . I studied and learned a lot about substitution. I learned a lot about improvisation. I learned a lot about synchronicity and a lot of good stuff. . . . The little bit I paid attention, I got a lot out of. And now, that's why I say, I wish I could kick myself for not having studied closer what he was telling me, because he was revealing these great secrets.[14]

"New York State of Mind"

As we've seen, Billy Joel's early works had leaned toward the eclecticism of the Beatles. Each of his albums had reached for this kind of stylistic variety in a decidedly impressive manner. Now, it was time for him to step up to the plate and give listeners a healthy serving of a style that he had yet to explore, but knew quite well—jazz. On "New York State of Mind," Joel speaks the language of jazz like a native son. On an interview for the program *Inside the Actors Studio,* Joel explained how the song's mood genuinely reflected the relief he felt when returning to New York after three years of working on the West Coast:

> I was moving back to New York. I landed at—I don't remember if it was LaGuardia or JFK, but I had to take a bus up to Highland Falls, a small town just south of West Point, on the west side of the Hudson River. And I'm riding on a Greyhound Bus—it was the Hudson River Line—and the idea started to come to me. . . . And I get to the house . . . ran up the stairs and started writing this song, and about an hour later had the whole song done, music and lyrics. I was so glad to be there and . . . I wanted to say I've been gone, I've been down, but I'm back.[15]

When hearing "New York State of Mind," the listener is struck by the way in which the song feels so familiar. However, it's not the familiarity experienced while listening to "Stardust" or "As Time Goes By." Rather, we are led to wonder if there might be a postmodern aesthetic at work here, something that is, in a sense, Beatlesque. Despite his love for the style, Joel must know deep down that the music he is referencing actually belongs to another generation. Thus, what he gives us in "New York State of Mind" is a retelling of "Georgia on My Mind" as it might have been reimagined by Paul McCartney for the Beatles' *The White Album*.[16]

"Summer, Highland Falls"

"Summer, Highland Falls" functions as a meditation on Joel's experiences while creating his first three albums in sunny California. By this time, he had extricated himself from his management deal with Artie Ripp and segued into a contract with Columbia Records. He'd been touring extensively as an opening act for some of the most respected artists in music, and was now headlining at venues all around the country. He was also recording with his own band, a group of talented musicians who came from his own cultural world. He had achieved all of this through perseverance, hard work, and a considerable amount of innate musical talent.

At the tender age of twenty-seven, it seemed that Joel had plenty to be happy about. So why, then, does this song sound so sad? In musical terms, Joel himself describes the emotional undercurrent that drove the composition of this song:

> I found a pattern with my left hand that was up-and-down, both in terms of the keyboard and the mood that it created. I knew I had something, but it lacked an element. Then I began knocking out a fast, arpeggiated pattern of "straight eights" with my right hand, almost like something out of Bach. I was trying to communicate that sometimes frantic, scurrying side of how we live our lives, and how we think about them.[17]

Although written on the East Coast shortly after Billy Joel's return to New York, "Summer, Highland Falls" bears the unmistakable trace of an L.A. sound, specifically that of singer-songwriter Jackson Browne.

In the mid-1970s, Browne had cornered the market on sensitive, confessional pop storytelling. His album *Late for the Sky* (1974) deftly employed a rustic hymn-like approach that lends a haunting authenticity to Browne's often-solemn musings on life, love, and mortality. At the time, the effect of his music was quite startling and could make contemporary artists like the Eagles sound kitschy by comparison. Since the opening phrase of "Summer, Highland Falls" echoes the verse melody of Jackson Browne's "These Days," it seems reasonable to assume that Joel was listening to, and in the case of "Summer, Highland Falls," being directly influenced by Browne's music.

The lyric explores human relationship in terms of the fundamental divide that exists between us all. According to Billy Joel, we are always looking across this chasm and attempting to provide the missing element for the other person in our lives. In the process, we experience a kind of emotional roller coaster that ultimately must take its toll on our psyches. This view is decidedly bleaker than those expressed in the lyrics of Jackson Browne, who would probably assert that a balance between ecstasy and despair is the best we can hope for. Billy Joel seems to disagree.

Regarding Billy Joel's earlier description of the up-and-down pattern of the piano line in the verse, the listener should also take note of the way he structures the musical setting in order to expand on the lyrical content. The opening chord lacks a third, that is, the qualifying note that determines whether or not a chord is major (happy) or minor (sad). It is sensible for the listener to assume that despite the missing note, the chord is major (happy). This is confirmed by the arrival of the second chord, the root of which provides the missing note (A) suggesting that the first chord was major (happy) after all.

However, the situation is complicated by the fact that this new chord seems sad (minor) in quality, but also contains additional elements from the first chord, which as we noted was major (happy). Thus, in the interplay between the text and the musical setting, happiness is layered on top of sadness, suggesting that the two states are always related. This provides an interesting contrast with the assertion made in the lyric that we must be in either one state (ecstasy) or the other (despair).

Stylistically, the song builds on the folk elements that were last heard in songs like "Everybody Loves You Now" and "Falling of the Rain" from *Cold Spring Harbor*, and "You're My Home" from *Piano Man*. In those songs, there was an ongoing attempt to translate the picked patterns associated with acoustic guitar into the arpeggiations associated with keyboard style. Here, Joel expands on that idea with a keyboard figuration seemingly derived from the first prelude of J.S. Bach's *Well-Tempered Clavier, Book I*. Such usage is interesting in that it serves to highlight the connections that can exist between musical genres that are seemingly remote.

"James"

The story of "James" is similar to the one presented in "Summer, Highland Falls," but not nearly as severe. Essentially, this is a bittersweet meditation on the road not taken, in which the main character asks an old friend how his life has turned out. We never do get a response, but the impression given is that the friend has opted for a more conventional lifestyle than the narrator. Although there is a countercultural bias that leans toward the legitimacy of the narrator's path, there is also an audible longing in his vocal that suggests he may be questioning his own choices. The listener is led to wonder if the narrator covets the nurturing that James received in pursuing an education. If so, his inquiry provides an ideal opportunity to consider what he himself has left behind.

The musical setting treats listeners to another serving of jazz-based elegance, most apparent in the sequence of falling major and minor seventh chords that are featured in the chorus. However, the figure of J. S. Bach also makes another appearance in the introduction and coda, played by Joel on the Fender Rhodes electric piano. This time, instead of employing figures derived from *The Well-Tempered Clavier*, Joel cleverly accesses gestures found in Invention No. 15 in B minor, BWV 786.

"James" constitutes an attempt to fuse classical and jazz into a coherent, yet richly eclectic sound. It also reinforces the notion that throughout his career, Billy Joel has been consistently interested in the synthesis of contrasting elements and ideas. In effect, he often seems to be rubbing one musical style against another in the hopes that the process might generate new meanings. In "James," the oppositional elements in the musical setting combine to create a dynamic and dramatic ground for the lyrical text.

"Prelude/Angry Young Man"

Although they'd long since confirmed their musical mastery, the Beatles drove the point home in 1969 with their final recorded work, *Abbey Road*. That remarkable album features a sequence of ostensibly unrelated tracks that display a sophistication and eloquence not normally associated with pop music. The *Abbey Road Medley*, as it has come to be called, is actually a three-movement work brimming with inventive musical development and considerable lyrical charm. Building on what Brian Wilson and the Beach Boys had achieved with *Pet Sounds* (1966), as well as their own landmark LP, *Sgt. Pepper's Lonely Hearts Club Band* (1967), the Beatles created an extended form in pop music that was at once traditional and progressive. Here, the group had laid down an implicit challenge to all those who came in their wake.

In the early 1970s, a number of progressive rock artists attempted to rise to the challenge of the *Abbey Road Medley*. Arguably, the most successful attempt was Elton John's "Funeral for a Friend/Love Lies Bleeding" from *Goodbye Yellow Brick Road* (1973). On that track, Elton melds a mournful instrumental with a power-pop song in the style of David Bowie to create what amounts to an eleven-minute prog-rock suite. Towards the end of the pop song section, Elton returns to the sparser textures of the instrumental with material that suggests the mourning process alluded to in the track's title is now complete. Gradually, he builds back into a restatement of the chorus hook of the pop song before triumphantly fading away into the distance.

Billy Joel had already proven that he could meet the Beatles' standard by prodigiously creating albums entirely on his own. He'd also been experimenting with expanded symphonic textures on tracks like "Tomorrow Is Today" from *Cold Spring Harbor* and "The Ballad of Billy the Kid" from *Piano Man*. Now, like Elton, he would begin to rise to the compositional challenge of the *Abbey Road Medley* by moving in the direction of extended form with "Prelude/Angry Young Man."

The "Prelude" to "Angry Young Man" opens with a bravura piano line of rapidly repeating sixteenth notes on middle C. As Joel readily points out, this motive references the Eyewitness News theme (WABC-TV, New York): "Actually, it's not hard to do. If you're a drummer—any drummer can do it. But people are like, 'Wow, how'd you do that?' And they try to do it with one hand. Actually, it sounds like Eyewitness News."[18] The Channel 7 Eyewitness News theme was originally written for the film *Cool Hand Luke* (1967), and the composer of that score was Lalo Schifrin. Born in Argentina in 1932, Schifrin was a key figure in the link between classical and jazz:

> [Schifrin] won a scholarship to the Paris Conservatoire, where he . . . studied with Olivier Messiaen. While in Paris he played with local

jazz artists and in 1955 represented Argentina in the third International Jazz Festival. On his return home he established himself as a composer, arranger, conductor and pianist who was equally at ease in popular, jazz and art-music circles. . . . Schifrin moved to New York in 1958, where he gained recognition as the pianist in Gillespie's jazz quintet (1960–62); he also recorded with other well-known jazz artists.[19]

Following the song's introduction, country and western elements make their final appearance on a Billy Joel recording. In the midst of a strident sequence of chords that suggests jazz fusion, we are reminded of a similar rhythmic pattern that occurs in the Coplandesque track, "The Ballad of Billy the Kid." This quality is enhanced by the subsequent appearance of harmonica to augment a bass line melody that evokes the American West. Joel's playing in this section also suggests the influence of Vince Guaraldi, who is perhaps best known as the composer/performer of "Cast Your Fate To the Wind" (1962) as well as the scores to the *Peanuts* cartoons.[20]

Following a restatement of the repeated piano line, the track segues into "Angry Young Man," an earnest folk song that hearkens back to "The Entertainer" from *Streetlife Serenade.* Like the earlier track, it features an active acoustic guitar as the lead rhythm instrument. This time, however, the pattern is highly syncopated with continuous offbeat accents under the lead vocal. The text looks satirically at the foibles of the eternally angry discontent that sees conspiracies at work throughout human culture. The character seems to be the last true believer and cannot let go of the past—something that Billy Joel, at this point, seems determined to do.

The song also features an anthemic passage that provides a strong contrast with the folk song model. The lyric articulates the notion that sooner or later, we must let go of idealism. The narrator describes his own experience of trying to let go in order to get down to the business of living his life. This section later repeats as an instrumental solo passage that features the Moog synthesizer. The anthemic quality remains, but the use of the Moog reaches toward progressive rock, most notably Emerson, Lake & Palmer. The "Prelude" then returns in a truncated form, thus working simultaneously as a return and a coda.[21]

POSTLUDE: BILLY JOEL AND JONI MITCHELL

On *Turnstiles*, Billy Joel was beginning to add jazz elements into his music. He also continued the process of color expansion that he began on *Streetlife Serenade*. As it turns out, he had a colleague who was also very interested in exploring these two elements as a part of her own musical language. That colleague was Joni Mitchell.

With regard to music and color, few artists of the 1970s accessed this idea in as full and unique a fashion as Joni Mitchell. From her first major pop success with "Both Sides Now" recorded by Judy Collins in 1968, she demonstrated an uncanny ability to use music and text to conjure up vivid and colorful imagery. In 1969, she recorded her own version of "Both Sides Now" on the album *Clouds*. Simple and unadorned, it had a unique charm all its own. That same album featured "Chelsea Morning," in which the lyrics seemed to elaborate on the colors created by "Both Sides Now."

A review of her albums from the early 1970s such as *Blue* (1971) and *For the Roses* (1972) reveals that Mitchell was gradually paring down the materials of her work, presumably to prepare for the growth that was soon to come. It was becoming evident that Mitchell was a visual artist who approached music like a painter. In an interview from the early 1990s, she described her process with regard to the relationship between sound and image:

> Well, all the arts are different. They engage different faculties. There are overlapping similarities. Certainly, aesthetics run through all of them. If your work is ornate musically, it's ornate in your painting. . . . And I ran into a sculptor, and I was drawing one of these very ornate things. He said, "That's nice." And I said, "No, it's not, I hate it." "Why do you hate it?" he said. I said, "It's too ornate." He said, "Oh, here, draw me and don't look at the paper." So I did, and it created a very bold and loose kind of line. And shortly after that, the adjectives began to fall away from my writing. The curlicues began to fall away; the grace notes began to fall away from the picking . . . the aesthetic shift took place across the board, but it started first with the eye and then the ears followed.[22]

A few months after Billy Joel released *Piano Man,* Joni Mitchell released *Court and Spark*. Here, she cultivated a new sound that incorporated a variety of her musical interests, including jazz. From the dreamy seascapes of "Help Me," to the flowing textures of "People's Parties," to the complex suite-like structure of "Down to You," the album's sweep and originality was truly remarkable. In addition, she seemed to have expanded the color field of her music, not just in terms of instrumental timbre, but also with a bright visual quality. The entire album seemed infused with sunlight.

Mitchell's follow-up to *Court and Spark, The Hissing of Summer Lawns* (1975), was even more colorful, with songs that flaunted their jazz-based ambitions. One track in particular conveyed an uncanny, lifelike quality. Titled "In France They Kiss on Main Street," it featured lyrics that cast a nostalgic look back at teenage dating rituals in the late 1950s. In the second verse there is a line concerning a dance hall, and two of the young ladies present are described as wearing "push-up brassieres." At first glance, this line might seem like an endearing but unremarkable brushstroke regarding two young women attempting to enhance their physical attractiveness. However, when music is added to the mix, something quite remarkable happens. The upward motion of the melody mimetically expresses the subject matter of the text, that is, the push-up brassieres worn by Gail and Louise!

Here, sight and sound merge to create a single, compelling metaphor for the human condition. Mitchell then intensifies this effect by having the melody move up by a single pitch at the end of the phrase. This helps emphasize the idea that the brassieres in question were of the push-up variety. It also suggests that Gail and Louise are manually adjusting their garments with a quick, yet discreet motion. A further element that helps reify the scene is the presence of a suspension in the underlying harmony that resolves downward just before the next phrase begins.

The effect Mitchell achieves here recalls Cole Porter's "Every Time We Say Goodbye," in which the chords and the text crash into one another just as the chord progression begins to parallel the lyric's description of "the change from major to minor." In Mitchell's song, musical elements that seem to sit comfortably within both jazz and folk rub up against the textual imagery to conjure a richly detailed cultural world. The context and character of Gail and Louise become instantly recognizable through this basic human gesture portrayed in song.

It appears that Joni Mitchell and Billy Joel have a lot in common. On her albums from the mid-1970s, Mitchell created coloristic effects that were rooted in her experience as a painter, and at times bordered on the cinematic. She had achieved this by paring down her musical materials, which then allowed her to explore jazz as a part of her sound. Billy Joel had also explored the possibilities of musical color and had been creating works like "The Ballad of Billy the Kid," which seemed to be reaching for cinematic effects. With *Turnstiles*, he had convincingly incorporated jazz gestures, and thus began to evolve a highly original compositional voice. He would now continue to explore these elements on his next two albums: *The Stranger* (1977) and *52nd Street* (1978).

4

THE STRANGER ON 52ND STREET

As we've seen, following his time in Southern California, Billy Joel returned to New York in order to reconnect with his cultural identity and his muse. In the process, he initiated a new phase in his work that resulted in the self-produced *Turnstiles*, arguably his finest collection of songs to date. However, although Joel did a serviceable job on the production, it was clear he would still need someone to fill the producer's chair. At this point, Elizabeth Weber Joel, his wife and now, manager, suggested that he work with Phil Ramone.[1]

ENTER PHIL RAMONE

Phil Ramone is regarded as one of the most important record producers of the twentieth century.[2] As a cofounder of A&R Studios in New York City, he seemed able to work in every genre and style, and was renowned for his ability to nurture new artists and help them find what they were looking for in their music. Born in South Africa, Ramone had come to the United States as a child and soon became a well-known prodigy on the violin, mentored by professors on the Julliard faculty. Throughout his early musical training, he also exhibited a fascination with sound recording as an art form.[3] Ramone described this period in his development during his keynote address for the 2008 Art of Record Production Conference at University of Massachusetts, Lowell:

By the time I was ten or eleven, at every school, including Julliard, I'd say, "Can I run the sound system?" And I learned, and I got invited to play, you know, in the section . . . I played some piece of a Mendelssohn concerto, I guess. It was the last page, as I recall, and it's very showy, and you think you're really good, but it set a pace for me to ask the engineers at RCA: What do I do? How can I play this better? How are you going to mike it? It started this idiot kind of thing that I was into, which was *sound*. [4]

Someone who was into *sound* was exactly what Billy Joel needed. From the beginning, the problem lay in the way that his music was being represented on vinyl. Of course, he'd had that previous bad experience with the mastering of *Cold Spring Harbor*. His next two albums, *Piano Man* and *Streetlife Serenade*, were clean and professional, but somewhat dull in their overall effect. The music didn't seem to jump off the record the way it should. Joel had bounced back with the self-produced *Turnstiles*, but there were still issues regarding sound quality that Phil Ramone would soon help remedy, as Don Evans points out:

I think that's what it is with *The Stranger*, and pretty much everything since. There's been a certain romantic vision . . . the whole sound picture is amazing. That's what hadn't really happened with Michael Stewart, and it didn't happen on *Turnstiles* either . . . I think they needed someone on the sessions other than Billy or the engineer. Someone who could ask questions like, "Why aren't those piano hammers hitting me in the face?" [5]

For his part, Ramone had been receptive to the idea of working with Billy Joel. He had gone to see him perform with his live band and listened closely to his first three albums. When the two finally met, he praised Joel's songs, but didn't shy away from pointing out the shortcomings of his recordings. He also said that he loved the sound and style of the group and told Billy that he would prefer to use them in the studio as opposed to session players. Joel was delighted with what he was hearing, and thus began his nine-year collaboration with Phil Ramone. [6]

Still, even though everything now seemed to be securely in place, there was an unspoken pressure coming from the executives at Columbia Records. After all, Joel's first three albums had not sold particularly well, and *Turnstiles* had only been a critical rather than a commercial success.

> Billy and I suffered because we'd not known each other but a couple of months, and then got to know each other really well. And they gave us about three weeks to do a whole album, but he didn't have enough songs. There was a PBS special on him and during an interview he said, "Phil never said this is my last chance, because the label had told Phil, 'If it doesn't work, he's out of here.'" And he said, "Thank God I didn't have that pressure."[7]

THE STRANGER (1977)

Overview

Artists who have had the opportunity to make more than one album begin to understand the importance of creating a unifying thread, some element that will help provide cohesion and unity within the recorded work. These threads need not be literal, such as the plot structure in a Broadway musical or the lyrical theme of a song cycle. They can be something as simple as a strategy employed to develop an album in terms of process. Consider the strategy employed by the Beatles during the making of *Sgt. Pepper's Lonely Hearts Club Band* (1967), as recounted by Paul McCartney:

> So I had this idea of giving the Beatles alter egos simply to get a different approach; then when John came up to the microphone or I did, it wouldn't be John or Paul singing, it would be the members of this band. It would be a freeing element. I thought we can run this philosophy through the whole album; with this alter-ego band, it won't be us making all that sound, it won't be the Beatles, it'll be this other band, so we'll be able to lose our identities in this.[8]

Sgt. Pepper isn't really a concept album. Instead, the unifying thread of the album was a creative strategy that allowed the Beatles to explore songs and characters in ways that might confound a more linear thematic approach. The various members of the group wore creative masks in order to achieve greater flexibility within the recording process. *The Stranger* aims for a similar kind of flexibility.

On his previous albums, Billy Joel had shown his talent for approaching a variety of everyday characters with a remarkable eye for detail. Phil Ramone described this quality in terms of its dramatic effect:

> Billy's lyrics had a distinct dramatic flair; his ideas, and the eloquent way he expressed them, were sophisticated. Songs such as "She's Always a Woman to Me," "Just the Way You Are," and "Everybody Has a Dream" allowed their stories to unfold effortlessly, and reflected sentiments that everyone could understand.[9]

In connection, we can also note that earlier Billy Joel songs like "Piano Man" and "Captain Jack" had each exhibited painterly qualities that distinguished Joel's work from many of his pop music contemporaries. During the aforementioned interview from the early 1990s (quoted in chapter 3), Joni Mitchell described how painters concern themselves with visual gestures that constitute "the residue of movement frozen in time." Musicians, through the use of sound, create gestures for motion itself. By applying painterly principles to musical forms, Joel succeeded in unfreezing the residue of movement, while at the same time retaining the painter's desire to preserve. The result was a gallery of images that danced in the liminal space between sight and sound. Now, he would take the process a step further.

Building on the dramatic and painterly qualities of Billy Joel's earlier works, *The Stranger* appears to develop along the lines of a classic Hollywood film. The visual qualities of the album's narrative are thus expanded via the incorporation of production ideas inspired by cinema. Assumedly, the specific model was film noir, a black-and-white style of filmmaking that flourished in the mid-twentieth century.[10] The worlds of film noir tend to portray the gradual move from the seeming moral clarity of prewar America toward the disturbing ambiguities of the atomic age. On *The Stranger*, Billy Joel and Phil Ramone create a sonic landscape of light and dark in which the characters of Brenda, Eddie, Mama Leone, Sergeant O'Leary, and Virginia all seem to inhabit and participate in a film noir narrative.

There are a number of precedents for the influence of cinematic technique on record production. The Beatles' *Revolver* (1966) features a remarkable track titled "Got to Get You into My Life." Largely writ-ten by Paul McCartney, this song was a tribute to the sound of Motown groups like the Supremes, the Four Tops, and the Temptations. At 1:49, just prior to the fadeout, an electric guitar played by George Harrison begins to emerge from the sound mass, chiming a repeating figure that echoes the strident horn section. Gradually, the volume of the guitar increases in relation to the other instruments in a manner that suggests we are zooming in on the fret board. Harrison then re-states the song's introductory riff with great precision in what amounts to an aural equivalent of a cinematic close-up.[11]

Also, consider the strange shimmering effect featured during the introduction to the song "Across 110th Street" by Bobby Womack. On this powerful example of early '70s R&B, organ and electric guitar play a syncopated groove that prepares the listener for the entrance of the lead vocal. At approximately 0:05, the organ descends into the next chord in a downward pitch bend that smears the auditory image. The effect is striking in that it tends to disorient the listener in the manner of a cinematic flashback.

Finally, there is Elton John's *Goodbye Yellow Brick Road* (1973), an album that uses images and ideas derived from the language of classic film to report on a culture steeped in escapist fantasy. In the title track, the diatonic hymn-like pattern of the verse shifts chromatically into a new key. In the process, it creates a musical corollary for the famous shift in *The Wizard of Oz* from black and white to color. The chorus that follows the transition has characteristics of both the diatonic verse and the chromatic transition and thus parallels the experiences of the film's main character, Dorothy Gale, who ultimately recognizes the connective threads that exist between her monochromatic life in Kansas and her multicolored trip to Oz.

As with *Sgt. Pepper's Lonely Hearts Club Band*, the story of *The Stranger* unfolds in a world of simultaneous happenings. The Beatles' theme on *Sgt. Pepper* seemed to concern the emergence of electric culture and the subsequent realities, good and bad, of total global in-volvement. In order to realize this idea, the band members put on masks that allowed them to escape the constrictive influence of corpo-rate identity and report more effectively on the world around them.

On *The Stranger* it is not Billy Joel, but the characters themselves, who are wearing the masks. They all live lives that coincide, but they are strangely isolated and alone, lost in the deep shadows of a film noir narrative. They each have aspirations, needs, and desires, but all they can show is the mask they want you to see. In the final analysis, the success of *The Stranger* can be measured in terms of the way these characters are portrayed in terms of their basic humanity.

"Movin' Out (Anthony's Song)"

The Stranger opens with "Movin' Out (Anthony's Song)," a song populated by an interesting collection of urban characters. The first is Anthony, a young man who works hard for a grocer in the hopes that someday, he will be able to move up to a better life. He is evidently being watched over by Mama Leone, a local customer who leaves him notes suggesting that he shouldn't wait, but move on right now to a better life while he's still young.[12] In contrast with Anthony's plight, we also have Sergeant O'Leary who walks a policeman's beat by day but works as a bartender by night. His goal is to save enough money to buy a luxury car that will fulfill the youthful dreams he left behind. Unwilling to settle for O'Leary's plight, Anthony resolves to take Mama Leone's advice, move to the country, and leave the city life behind.

According to Billy Joel, the lyric of "Movin' Out (Anthony's Song)" was unconsciously written to the melody and chord progression of Neil Sedaka's "Laughter in the Rain" (1974).[13] Joel also claims that he did not like Sedaka's song, and was rather irritated by the fact that he now had to come up with an entirely new melody to a pre-existing lyric. Nevertheless, this process seems to have allowed him the opportunity to stretch his creativity. The new chord progression reworks sequential elements from the verse of "James," while the active, melodic bass line hearkens back to "Captain Jack." Joel has also asserted that the spirit of this new melody was inspired by the vocal style of Jon Anderson, the lead singer of Yes.[14]

Another noteworthy feature of "Movin' Out (Anthony's Song)" is the influence of the sound of the Beatles. We've already discussed the group's inspiration regarding the production concept of *The Stranger*. On this track, the compressed energy of the rhythm section, the melodically active electric guitar lines played by Steve Khan, and the chirpy backing vocals overdubbed by Billy Joel himself, all display the marked influence of the mid-'60s Beatles style. Nevertheless, the song maintains its own musical identity throughout. Rather than sounding like a Beatles imitator, Joel once again integrates the group's influence in a manner that serves to enhance his own distinctive artistic vision.

"The Stranger"

After setting the scene for the various characters portrayed in the opening track, *The Stranger* now moves on to an examination of the inner lives of those characters. The surfaces that typify personality and identity are described here as masks that we all wear. The narrator resists the temptation toward cynicism and concludes that hiding behind a mask is an inevitable part of the human experience. Thus, we should not be afraid to soldier on, do our best, and give others the space that they need to do the same.

Musically, Joel pares down his elements to create a stark, compelling mental landscape that is the realm of the main character, the Stranger. The instrumental theme that begins the track is arguably a cliché, that is, a routine minor-key melody that moves between the mournful and the mysterious. In spite of this, the theme benefits greatly from the cinematic resonance it generates through a shared cultural reference. The main body of the song continues in the same mournful tone, but this time with a more active and aggressive rhythmic stance. This is especially evident in the guitar riff that deftly mixes blues, jazz, and twentieth-century quartal harmony. Otherwise, the piece is rather mundane in terms of its basic materials, but Joel actually uses this to his advantage.

Building on the structural design of "Prelude/Angry Young Man," Joel brackets both sides of the track's main section with the instrumental theme. This allows him to maintain the intensity and keep the song driving forward. On first listen, the move from the opening instrumental into the main body of the song is more convincing than the transition back into the instrumental at the end. However, it should also be noted that there, Phil Ramone is employing a crossfade, which gives the impression of experiencing the aural equivalent of a familiar cinematic effect. At the same time, it demonstrates the use of recording technology as an integral part of the compositional process.

"Just the Way You Are"

Despite the many romantic associations for this song, the lyrics seem to be suggesting something rather pitiful. The main character/narrator wishes to keep someone exactly as she is. In other words, he seems to be rejecting change, and thus rejecting the possibility that his lover could develop, grow, and move on without him. At the same time, the listener could also read the text as a response to someone's neurotic desire to compulsively change. There are two people involved in this situation. Like the characters in "Summer, Highland Falls," they stand over the chasm that exists between them, trying to make a lasting and meaningful connection. In that sense, we could say that there is something healthy going on here. Perhaps it is an honest desire to stabilize and not fall victim to the ecstatic highs and crushing lows of romantic love.

The musical setting renders a microcosm of the jazz pop scene that was a key feature of 1970s culture. As on "James" from *Turnstiles*, the keyboard sound references the title track from Paul Simon's jazz pop classic, *Still Crazy After All These Years* (1975). In the process, it also connects with the work of jazz fusion artists like Chick Corea and Bob James. The most overt and elegant reference to jazz is the extraordinary alto sax solo played by the great Phil Woods. Interestingly, Woods had also played on a key track from the aforementioned Simon album. There, at the end of "Have a Good Time," he does an elaborate bebop solo that works as the tag/coda of the song. Producer Phil Ramone describes how this came about:

> There's a song, "Have a Good Time" on Paul Simon's record [*Still Crazy After All These Years*] for which I called him [Phil Woods], and he drove all the way from Pennsylvania to New York City. He said, "What do you want on it?" (Snaps fingers in a quick tempo) I said, "B flat. One minute. Play!" He tells the story to this day. I mean he just played some great bebop and I used it as the tail fadeout. . . . What happened when we did it on the stage with Paul Simon a year later is we got two great players, one of them was Dave Sanborn. And they wrote out every note of the way Phil did it, and they did it as a two-saxophone duet.[15]

Woods's solo on "Just the Way You Are" is more completely integrated into the overall sound. Rather than just playing a tag as he does on the

Simon record, he is mixed as a full part of the ensemble. In the process, his beautiful solo serves to highlight elements of the composition that link up traditional jazz with jazz fusion and pop.

With regard to production, there is an important pop single of the 1970s that is not usually discussed in relation to "Just the Way You Are." The song is titled "I'm Not in Love," and the band is 10cc. In 1975, this track was considered to be a breakthrough in terms of the potential of sound recording as a viable art form. Somewhat jazz inspired in that it also featured a Fender Rhodes piano, "I'm Not in Love" was a postmodern love song that expanded on methods used by the Beatles on "Tomorrow Never Knows" (1966) and "Revolution 9" (1968). On those tracks, tape loops were fed into a recording console that was effectively "played" like an instrument during the final mixing session.[16]

"Revolution 9" and "Tomorrow Never Knows" were primarily expressionistic works by design and overall effect. With "I'm Not in Love," the members of 10cc took this process a step further. Using their own voices, they multitracked each note of the chromatic scale onto an enormous tape loop and layered them onto sixteen-track analog tape. Then, during the mixing process, they effectively turned the recording console into a makeshift organ, creating actual harmonies as a support for the main body of the song. Composer and lead singer Eric Stewart explains:

> Then, all four of us manned the control desk, and each of us had three or four faders to work with. We moved the faders up and down and changed the chords of the 13 chromatic scale notes as the chords of the song changed—13 tracks on a 16-track tape, fed through the control desk faders, back out of the master fader and onto that stereo pair of open tracks that was left free on the 16-track machine. . . . Luckily we got it. We got it just right. We very, very quickly got the lead vocal down and then we sat there, I tell you seriously, for about three days, just listening to this thing.[17]

The aesthetic effect they created was truly remarkable, and doesn't seem to have been lost on Billy Joel. The vocal harmonies on "Just the Way You Are" suggest the influence of the ethereal voices created by 10cc on "I'm Not in Love." They create a curious atemporal effect reminiscent of cinematic flashback. In addition to the vocals, a recurring string oscillation that recalls a similar effect on the Beatles' "A Day in the Life" intensifies the overall sense of dislocation. In tandem with the qualities achieved on the album's previous tracks, these brushstrokes help prepare the listener for the elaborate and extended flashback sequence of *The Stranger*'s centerpiece, "Scenes from an Italian Restaurant."

"Scenes from an Italian Restaurant"

The career of the Beatles came to an end with the release of their final recorded work, *Abbey Road* (1969). As previously discussed, the highlight of that album was a sequence of seemingly unrelated song fragments that together have come to be known as the *Abbey Road Medley*. "Scenes from an Italian Restaurant" can trace its inspiration back to that work, as Billy Joel points out:

> The format of this songwriting was inspired by a chunk of material on the B-side of *Abbey Road*. "Anybody who's familiar with that B-side has probably figured out by now it's a series of song fragments," says Billy. "The Beatles would come into a recording session, and John would go, 'I've got a bit of this,' and Paul would say, 'I've got a piece of this,' and then George Martin would say, 'Well, let's stitch it all together and we can make this work.' It adds up to a sixteen-minute medley, and I thought it was brilliant."[18]

The spirit of the entire medley informs "Scenes from an Italian Restaurant," but it seems to most closely parallel the final section, titled "Golden Slumbers/Carry That Weight/The End." It also differs from the medley in an interesting way. Specifically, it features a full return of the opening section. Here, Joel builds on what he'd already been attempting with "Prelude/Angry Young Man" and "The Stranger." Specifically, he opts to use the opening section as a means of effectively bracketing the inner sections of a work.

Section 1, "The Italian Restaurant Song": In the opening section, we encounter a middle-aged couple who are contemporaries of the characters we originally met in "Movin' Out (Anthony's Song)." The setting is a quaint Italian restaurant where they've come to dine and reminisce about their journey—how they got here and what they chose to leave behind. The instrumental setting expresses a certain amount of nobility that underscores their connection to one another. Soon, the music begins to morph as the couple embarks on a memory/time trip. They begin to journey back toward an encounter with their younger selves.[19]

Section 2, "Things Are Okay in Oyster Bay": The dreamy transition into section 2 evokes the score of a romantic Hollywood film. It paves the way for a bouncy tune for piano and voice that is filled with the optimistic energies of young adulthood. The singer, presumably the younger incarnation of the man in the restaurant, describes his career achievements and his ability to care for his family. However, in the middle of the verse he begins to reveal an emerging distance between himself and his partner. Was he initially wearing a mask? Before things completely fall apart, he tries to remind her of their days spent together on the "Village Green," presumably a local teenage hangout. This section then begins to morph into an instrumental transition in the spirit of a New Orleans jam session.[20]

Section 3, "The Ballad of Brenda and Eddie": This section recounts the tale of a teenage couple, their initial romance, and its ultimate dissolution as foreshadowed in section 2. Brenda and Eddie are high school sweethearts who have tried to make a go of it with little to go on. Their origins are working class, and so we can assume they are not particularly well educated. Once the realities of everyday life set in, it's clear that they don't have the necessary skills to make their relationship work. The lively rock 'n' roll setting of the text is at once appropriate to the time period (1950s–1960s) and an ironic contrast to the sadness of the story.[21]

We now build to the final transition, a descending scalar passage that gradually changes the mode from G major to F major, the key of the opening section. Initially, this passage might seem to go on a bit too long when compared with a similar transition in the last verse of the Beatles' "A Day in the Life" from *Sgt. Pepper's Lonely Hearts Club Band* (1967). However, looking more closely, we see that Joel needs a much longer transition here, since he is now traveling back to the present! The preceding sections were journeys back in time/memory, so he has to allow for the long journey home. The end of the passage is characterized by a gradual slowing down of tempo as we approach the triumphant return of section 1.

Section 1 (reprise), "The Italian Restaurant Song": We now find ourselves in the present and understand that the couple in the restaurant is, in fact, Brenda and Eddie. Their encounter at the beginning of the song was a reunion in which they were coming to terms with their shared history. The musical setting is even more magisterial than before, suggesting that in spite of our individual sorrows, our basic humanity survives. This return is followed by the musical transition initially heard between section 1 and section 2. Now, however, it has been repurposed as coda. Following a full musical close, we fade to black.[22]

The use of the phrase "fade to black" is of course deliberate. It emphasizes the point that "Scenes from an Italian Restaurant" constitutes persuasive evidence that with *The Stranger*, Billy Joel and Phil Ramone were incorporating cinematic techniques into their production process. In a sense, the track works as a film within a film, an extended flashback sequence in which the lives of the characters are explored in a series of cross-dissolves that are themselves characteristic of human memory. Informed by the art of the film score and the medium of film itself, Billy Joel and his collaborators succeeded in creating musical corollaries for sweeping cinematic effects.

52ND STREET (1978)

Overview

With *The Stranger*, Billy Joel had the production style he needed. He now had a framework for his songs, and had learned to produce and arrange them in such a way so that the whole was greater than the sum of its parts. He had finally stepped into the big leagues with a collection that could easily be measured against the work of great artists like the Beatles. So, what would be the next move? Phil Ramone described how he and Joel resolved to face the challenge together:

> I mean I used to try to inspire Billy because with the first album [*The Stranger*] being a big hit, I knew they were going on the road, and I knew, as a result, that he wouldn't write. Sometimes he'd call me from the road. . . . And he said, "How we gonna make the second album?" I said, "You want me? I'll face the same problem you will." He said, "Yeah, we should try."[23]

Since evidence suggested that *The Stranger* conceptually incorporated cinematic elements derived from film noir and was thus in black and white, it must have seemed logical to take that idea and go into full color. Thus, Joel could effectively "colorize" a new set of characters similar to those featured on *The Stranger*, and continue the story in the form of a sequel. The characters of *52nd Street* are varied, interesting, and above all, colorful. Little Geo, Angelina, and Rosalinda are all on hand, dreaming of Cuban skies, life on the West Coast, and holidays in the sun. There are also exotic locations like Park Avenue and Elaine's Bar and Restaurant that provide a stark contrast to the lives of the characters of *52nd Street*, who tend to drink in sports bars and live anonymous lives out in Shantytown.

This is all well and good, but simply continuing the story of *The Stranger* in living color would not be enough to make the new album work. Clearly, there would have to be more. Thus, Joel and Ramone decided to reach back to *Turnstiles* and use musical tropes derived from American jazz to expand and develop their sound. Since it allowed for a further expansion of instrumentation, this stylistic choice was fitting for an attempt to bring the world of *The Stranger* into full color. Initially, Billy Joel was hesitant about whether or not they could actually pull this idea off, but Phil Ramone urged him to try:

> "Why shouldn't you experiment a bit, at least on a few songs, if not a whole album?" I asked. "It's okay to create a jazz kind of mood. You can do it credibly because you've written a song called "Zanzibar," and at the very end there are jazz riffs. Those phrases are a nod to all of the great jazz artists you heard while you were growing up." I convinced him to chance the dramatic, and *52nd Street*—the second record that Billy and I made together, in 1978—took his music in a new direction.[24]

The characters of *52nd Street* seem to mesh with the underlying message that jazz is an important expression of human creativity and dignity. To his credit, however, Ramone never allows these themes to get heavy or pretentious. From the raunchy down-home strut of the title track to the cool, easy swing of "Zanzibar," the stylistic gestures are assured, yet accessible. A keen awareness of Steely Dan echoes throughout the production, and although Joel's swaggering persona lacks the smoky authenticity of a Donald Fagen, it does possess a sweep and grandeur all its own.

"My Life"

"My Life" tells the story of an old friend who has evidently decided to follow Billy Joel's example, put everything on the line, and move to the West Coast in search of his dreams. Although somewhat cynical about his friend's chances, Joel still supports his right to determine his own future without pressure from family or cultural expectations. He favors the idea that everyone should have an opportunity to try and should have the courage to somehow make their dreams come true.

Ultimately, the opening story pales in importance compared to the message from the narrator himself. The friend has told him what he has planned, and this triggers something from the narrator's own experience in breaking free. The message is important enough that he feels the need to pass along what he has learned to the listener. Although it expresses a very noble sentiment, the story somehow feels incomplete in that it starts off well, and just keeps ending, and ending, and ending . . .

The musical setting of "My Life" really saves the day and explains why the song was the first and most successful single from *52nd Street*. It compensates for any lyrical shortcomings that may be present with an interesting blend of musical gestures derived from mid- to late '70s pop. The tune is decidedly McCartneyesque and is therefore very accessible. It descends in a smooth, catchy melodic pattern that is impossible to resist. The rocking octave bass pattern and its strong reliance on the bass drum seems to connect with disco as well as the keyboard-driven pop of "Lido Shuffle" (1977) by Boz Scaggs, minus the swing.[25]

There is also a remarkable single chord in the introduction that becomes a pop hook all by itself. Described as a ninth chord (C9), this jazz-derived gesture seems to evoke the intro to Steely Dan's "Kid Charlemagne," albeit in a slightly altered form. Perhaps more significant is the fact that the chord seems to reference the antepenultimate harmony (D-flat ninth) from the verse of the Bee Gees' "How Deep Is Your Love" from *Saturday Night Fever* (1977). At that point in their career, the Bee Gees were reaping the benefits from having expanded their British folk pop style with American R&B. With this one subtle brushstroke, Joel simultaneously referenced state-of-the-art pop rock (Bee Gees) and jazz pop (Steely Dan)—but there was much more to come.

"Half a Mile Away"

On this delightfully appealing track, Billy Joel accesses the jazz-based television scores of the 1960s and 1970s. "Half a Mile Away" features a sharp horn orchestration from Dave Grusin that could work well within the context of a gritty urban drama. Here, it is used to explore the lives of characters struggling to create meaning and purpose in their lives.

We first hear of Little Geo, the singer's good friend and confidant with whom he spends his spare time on the edges of polite society. Then, there is Mamma, the mother that he clearly loves, but must find a way to get around in order to find some measure of fulfillment with his friends. Finally, we have Angelina, a young woman who offers the singer the very real possibility of redemption through her acceptance of who he really is. It's interesting to consider that the names Little Geo, Angelina, and even Mamma have a decided Latin connotation. Thus, there is the strong implication that they come from the world of *The Stranger*, the world of Mama Leone, Anthony, and Brenda and Eddie.

Although the lively arrangement makes this all sound rather exciting and fun, there is also an element of danger that gives life to the story. In his musical setting, Joel uses harmonic turnarounds derived from jazz practice to effectively create a sense of pathos. As a result, we can feel the pain of these characters. They suffer and struggle, celebrate and mourn. Through his musical setting, Joel gets the listener to experience those emotions in a powerful and profound way.

"Zanzibar"

"Zanzibar" sets up a seeming dichotomy between a main character who acts as narrator and the various cultural realities that he observes at his neighborhood hangout. Here, Joel offers listeners a remarkably accurate rendering of a metropolitan sports bar, circa 1978–1979. The working-class customers on hand are beginning to realize that their dreams of upward mobility are slowly slipping away. They never really made it into the middle class, and the economy is now in decline. In some ways, they portend the kinds of characters we'll be seeing on *The Nylon Curtain* (1982), four years and two albums later.

In any case, the focus of the main character/narrator bounces between the customers in attendance, the images he sees on the TV screen(s), and the mundane details of his own life. He mentions Muhammad Ali, Pete Rose, and the Yankees, as well as the effects of melodrama on the human psyche. This is all envisaged in high contrast with his own reality. So far, he doesn't have a lot to show: a car inherited from his father, a tab at the bar, and presumably, a decent job. He does, however, have a jazz guitar.

"Zanzibar" is probably the most important track on *52nd Street* in terms of unifying the character-driven concept of *The Stranger* and the jazz process threads of *Turnstiles*. Here, Joel stresses the connection between the song's characters and jazz music as a vital human activity. The main character here is clinging to his jazz guitar, indicating that he places a great deal of importance on music as a form of expression that is significant and unique. It may be the reason he's making connections with the waitress working at Zanzibar, who may like him because he wants to be a musician. Thus, we get a sense of continuity, the possibility of posterity, and the notion that even when hard times are upon us, there's hope.

The chorus of "Zanzibar" features a driving straight eighth note rhythm pattern and melodic bass line similar to those that grounded the verse of "Movin' Out (Anthony's Song)." The setting for the verse creates additional references to the work of Steely Dan. The chord progression here seems to be reaching for the kind of jazz-derived harmonic sophistication the listener finds on *The Royal Scam* (1976) and *Aja* (1977). Still, despite his interest in complex and exotic cluster chords, Joel seems unwilling to let go of the rhythmic power of rock 'n' roll. Thus, with "Zanzibar," he aims for a negotiation between piano-driven rock and traditional jazz. The latter is especially evident on the extended free-form solo performed by jazz trumpet great, Freddie Hubbard.

On *The Stranger*, producer Phil Ramone had contracted saxophone legend Phil Woods to enhance "Just the Way You Are" with jazz-derived musical gestures. In the case of "Zanzibar," Ramone suggested something similar but even more integrated:

> The theme offered us an expansive forum for experimentation; what emerged was a solid pop tune adorned with tasteful elements of hot and cool jazz. A particular highlight is the song's bridge, where a dreamy interlude (featuring keyboards and vibes) erupts into an unexpected jazz trumpet solo by Freddie Hubbard. Underscoring the

passage is a driving, ascending/descending bass line, which lends it an urgency that's irresistibly sexy.[26]

The interlude on keyboards and vibes that Ramone describes employed a series of quartal chords that are characteristic of artists like Chick Corea and Weather Report. These, in combination with the trumpet solo that follows, helped push the track beyond the confines of pop and into the realm of jazz fusion.

In the final analysis, "Zanzibar" can be regarded as the logical successor to "Scenes from an Italian Restaurant." There, Joel successfully employed structural techniques derived from the medium of cinema and the music of the Beatles to create a viable extended form. With "Zanzibar," he succeeds in stretching the boundaries of the pop song format through a skillful blending of musical genres. In the process, he unifies the various elements that form the foundation of *52nd Street*. In an interview with pianist Judy Carmichael for the radio program *Jazz Inspired*, Joel commented on the experience of recording this track:

> We played a track called "Zanzibar," where Freddie Hubbard played the trumpet. And we broke into this kind of free-form, jazz, improvisational solo. [Mimics the riff vocally] And . . . the groove was fantastic. We finished doing that recording and we all looked at each other and said, "Now, we're grown-ups." You know, 'cause only grown-ups play like that.[27]

"Rosalinda's Eyes"

The text of "Rosalinda's Eyes" weaves the characters and cultures of *52nd Street* into a compelling human portrait. The narrator is a working musician who takes any gig he can get in order to survive. In the process, he brings happiness and joy to those who hear him play. We learn that he is a Latin jazz musician, but are led to wonder just how much he is truly appreciated for his skills. Even so, the listener comes to understand that his craft is not only an enjoyable activity; it also makes an important contribution to the culture at large.

As the story unfolds, we get the sense that this musician is struggling to keep his art alive. He keeps faith in knowing that his wife Rosalinda understands his struggle and supports him in his efforts. She also helps him remember the beauty of Cuba, the country of his birth. This and the song's title combine to convey autobiographical elements in the text, as Billy Joel explains:

> It was kind of a romantic notion, and it told the story of a guy who's got music in his hands—*I'll be home, I'll be back, I'm always searching for my Cuban skies.* Because my old man lived in Cuba for a couple of years, I just folded in some bits and pieces of what I knew about my family background and romanticized that situation. [28]

The musical setting of "Rosalinda's Eyes" provides colors that are consistent with the thematic elements presented in the text. The introduction consists of a series of ambiguously minimalist whole-tone cluster chords played on an electric piano that evokes the sounds of a marimba. This is followed by a sparse verse melody supported by a baroque-style harmonic sequence. The sequence is distinguished by the fact that the chords are voiced in the manner of jazz pianist Bill Evans. Thus, Joel layers the two approaches (baroque/classical and jazz), one over the other.

Although somewhat disguised by the active rhythm parts, the chorus of "Rosalinda's Eyes" displays anthemic qualities that were present in earlier songs like "Tomorrow Is Today" and "I've Loved These Days." Once again, a traditionally conceived form is superimposed with an element derived from jazz—in this case, Latin percussion. Taking things a bit further, we also have an additional section that doubles as instrumental break/development. Consistent with verse and chorus, this new section employs chromatic harmony to arrive at some surprising jazz-based musical ideas that suggest the influence of Bob James. The expansive melody of this section is played on a sopranino recorder, at once evoking the timbral richness of classical music and the authenticity of folk.

"Rosalinda's Eyes" may not be as dramatic or as exciting as "Zanzibar," but it has a unique energy and charm. This is especially evident in its attempts to integrate jazz harmony within a classically conceived musical structure. Since the chromaticism of jazz tends to challenge the directed tonal motion of high classicism, the listener might think that the situation is fundamentally irresolvable. However, on another level, a resolution to this "problem" may well be beside the point. What Billy Joel really may have been after was not a new form, but a release of energy.

In the book *From Cliché to Archetype* (1970), Marshall McLuhan and Wilfred Watson assert that a cliché, that is, a repeatable process, "is charged with the accumulations of corporate energy and perception." They also stress that in order to "release energy the cliché needs the encounter of another cliché."[29] In this regard, we can assert that the jazz process and classical music have each accumulated a sizeable charge of energy within them through their repeated use. Thus, Joel's seeming attempts to incorporate these two processes into a unique and original style may actually be a camouflage. As an intuitive artist, he may simply have wanted to rub the styles together in order to release the powerful energies contained in each.

POSTLUDE: BILLY JOEL AND PAUL SIMON

It is worth considering Billy Joel's work in relation to Paul Simon. Both are baby boomers that grew up close, but not too close to Manhattan: Paul Simon in Kew Gardens, Queens, and Billy Joel in Hicksville, Long Island. Both evolved into natural storytellers, and several of Joel's early compositions—"Falling of the Rain," "Why Judy Why," and "You're My Home"—seem to bear the influence of Simon & Garfunkel. In the 1970s, Joel would often cover Simon's solo song "Still Crazy after All These Years" during live performances. More importantly, both artists shared a producer, Phil Ramone, who helped each of them in their efforts to develop their music beyond the stylistic confines of rock 'n' roll.

Paul Simon's early work is derived primarily from the language of rock 'n' roll. He had his first taste of success in 1957 with "Hey, School-girl," recorded with neighbor and friend Art Garfunkel as the duo Tom and Jerry.[30] The record was a minor hit and led to Simon working at New York's Brill Building, where talented hopefuls like Carole King and Gerry Goffin would try to write songs for established commercial artists of the day.[31] For a short time, Paul Simon was a Brill Building songwriter, but he wasn't a particularly good one.[32] Still, the experience gave him an appreciation for the nuances of the craft:

> You know, I think good songs are all about sound, I think that's what
> music is about. And the songwriter is listening to hear whether he or

she is creating a sound that has some meaning. Unless you're writing strictly on a commercial basis, I mean, unless you're being a hack— even there, a good hack has to have some kind of sensitivity. . . . I couldn't do it, and so I think that's the first time I moved to England, in 1963.[33]

Simon's move to England allowed him to explore and incorporate the folk music forms he heard there. This influence, along with the early rock 'n' roll that he'd heard as a teenager, resulted in songs that were relatively straightforward in terms of their musical materials. Upon returning to the United States, Simon reteamed with Art Garfunkel and began to ride the folk music wave to great success.[34] However, with the breakup of Simon & Garfunkel, his music began to take an interesting turn toward a jazz-based chromaticism. Elements of this coming change were already evident on *Bridge Over Troubled Water*, as pointed out by music scholar Walter Everett:

> An experimental composition, "So Long, Frank Lloyd Wright," on his last album before the break with Garfunkel . . . points to an early interest in chromaticism that subsequently matured through the 1970s, gaining in intensity with the tonally adventurous 1973 recording *There Goes Rhymin' Simon* and peaking in the 1975 album *Still Crazy after All These Years*.[35]

As Everett points out, Simon's work on both of these albums was adventurous in its exploration of a musical language derived from American jazz. In that regard, he was fortunate to have a producer like Phil Ramone collaborating with him on his recordings. So, was this endeavor successful? The answer is yes, often. At times, however, it seems that he was at a disadvantage in terms of instrumental technique. He certainly played the guitar in a skillful and pianistic fashion, but further development of his music using the more complex chord structures he was interested in was simply beyond his abilities on the instrument.

Billy Joel was also interested in the expansion of the popular musical language through jazz. At this point, he did not yet possess Simon's track record as a songwriter, but his primary instrument was the piano. Thus, the kind of harmonic complexity Paul Simon had been reaching for in his mid-'70s music was arguably more accessible to Billy Joel. In that light, it seems reasonable to assert that on his early to mid-1970s albums made in collaboration with Phil Ramone, Paul Simon began to expand the language of popular music with jazz. He then, in effect, passed the baton to Billy Joel who, with Ramone's help, would continue the process.

5

GENRE GAMES

By 1978, Billy Joel had racked up a list of professional accomplish-
ments that would be the envy of any musical artist. With *The Stranger*,
he and Phil Ramone had successfully employed production strategies
similar to those spearheaded by the Beatles on *Sgt. Pepper's Lonely
Hearts Club Band*. On "Scenes from an Italian Restaurant," the centerpiece of *The Stranger*, Joel had risen to the challenge set down by the
medley on the second side of *Abbey Road*. With *52nd Street*, the follow-up to *The Stranger*, he had taken the baton from Paul Simon regarding jazz influence on pop music and, in the process, had established
himself as the pre-eminent pop songwriter of his generation. What was
left to achieve?

Commenting on the Beatles' arrival in America in 1964 and their
subsequent career, critic and author Dave Marsh pointed out:

> The Beatles had not only arrived, they had arrived complete. They
> would not get better in the six years left to them, because there
> simply wasn't much better to get. What they did, instead, and to their
> everlasting credit, was become more sophisticated, take the same
> idea and never shy away from its complexities. But *better*? You don't
> improve on "I Want to Hold Your Hand" . . . you just elaborate.[1]

In the late 1970s, Billy Joel had arrived complete. Essentially, there
was nowhere left to go. Punk rock artists of that era were seeking to
displace the musical dinosaurs of the past by breaking the music back
down to its basic components. Through his attempts to match the

achievements of such dinosaurs, Billy Joel had, in effect, become one of them. With the six albums left to him, he would continue to elaborate on his musical achievements, but never truly surpass them.

GLASS HOUSES (1980)

Overview

By the time Billy Joel had finished touring to promote *52nd Street*, the cultural consensus concerning the incorporation of jazz into popular music was beginning to break down. With the release of *Mingus* (1979), Joni Mitchell had miscalculated the willingness of her pop audience to sit still for sophisticated musical hybrids. Clearly, the direction of the emerging aesthetic was toward simplicity rather than sophistication. In this regard, Steely Dan would soon stumble with *Gaucho* (1980), an album that missed the cultural wave of its era just as assuredly as their previous record *Aja* (1977) had caught it.

Billy Joel's response to this gradual shift away from the blending of jazz and pop was to temporarily retreat into the past. Like Paul McCartney, he became a "backwards traveller," eagerly retrieving the musical languages of prior cultural landscapes in order to sustain the kind of sophistication he valued so highly. At the same time, the punk/new wave movement was advocating a return to the more direct and less pretentious approach epitomized by early rock 'n' roll. After all he had achieved, Billy Joel suddenly had to prove himself once again.

His first effort in this regard was an album called *Glass Houses*. There, under the guise of a harder-edged, punk-influenced sound, he subtly sought to reveal the primary influence of this newly energized musical landscape—the Beatles. His strategy was very astute. A number of newer artists like Squeeze, the Cars, and Elvis Costello had already been attempting to incorporate musical ideas and gestures derived from the Beatles into their recordings. In keeping with this trend, Billy Joel opted to do the same.

"You May Be Right"

Glass Houses opens with "You May Be Right," a song that tells the story of a man who is recovering from a night of heavy partying. This fellow is now in the process of trying to convince the woman he loves that his rowdy and reckless behaviors are not really as dangerous as they might seem. He tells her this is how he lets off steam, and that it may well be an important way to maintain his mental health. He also implies that this unpredictable behavior provides an effective contrast to her more respectable and sober way of life. Further, he claims that his unpredictability may well be what attracted her to him in the first place.

In terms of the musical setting, "You May Be Right" purports to reference the rebellious and rocking style of the Rolling Stones, and with regard to the performance itself, this is certainly the case. However, as we look/listen closer, we realize that the material Joel is using is derived largely from the music of the Beatles. In its musical setting, the song attempts to fuse elements from two Beatles songs, one by John Lennon and the other by George Harrison.

Following the sound of breaking glass, a resilient electric guitar opens the track. The guitar's riff is a variation on the distinctive Beatles guitar sound of the mid-1960s, and the model seems to be "I Want to Tell You" from *Revolver* (1966). While Harrison's riff is expansive and complex, Joel's variation creates a more compact, obsessively repeating pattern that perfectly grounds his protagonist's need to unwind. The chord progression of the latter part of the verse evokes the hook from "Help!" (1965), suggesting perhaps that the narrator is hiding some personal trauma behind his reckless behavior.

"Don't Ask Me Why"

The lyrics address the same issues that were explored in "Big Shot," the opening track from *52nd Street* (1978). However, while that lyric was scathing in its indictment of a character that partakes of all the perks the New York nightlife has to offer, we now get a more sympathetic view of the situation. Many of us have tried to move from simplicity toward a more sophisticated lifestyle by seeking out the finer things in life. Eventually, however, we tend to come back around to the innocence that is arguably the source of our basic humanity. The lyric explores this fundamentally human circularity with a knowing yet affectionate humor.

The musical setting of "Don't Ask Me Why" refers to the compositional style of Paul McCartney within the context of an Afro-Cuban rhythmic groove. The McCartney influence is particularly evident in the voice leading of the chord progression, which is seemingly modeled on "Blackbird" from the Beatles' *White Album* (1968). However, Billy Joel also takes the opportunity to integrate elements from jazz by using an altered E minor seventh chord at the end of each refrain. This kind of altered chord is a common feature of jazz, but in conventional music theory, it would likely be regarded as a by-product of the underlying motion of the voices. Thus, within the context of Joel's oeuvre, the chord can be viewed as a stylistic pivot that exists simultaneously within the respective worlds of classical and jazz.

"Through the Long Night"

Glass Houses comes to a close with a gentle ballad, "Through the Long Night." An evident reference to the Welsh folk song "All Through the Night," the track demonstrates Billy Joel's remarkable mastery of musical technique. The intriguing lyric describes the singer's quiet devotion to his lover as he attempts to comfort her. As the song progresses, the listener begins to wonder exactly what it is that troubles her, but this is never revealed. Perhaps the singer knows what has happened, but he does not seem to care. He understands that the most important thing he can do for her now is to simply provide support.

In terms of its musical setting, "Through the Long Night" was another step forward for Billy Joel. On his early albums, he could often be heard emulating the acoustic guitar with piano arpeggiations. Songs such as "Falling of the Rain" from *Cold Spring Harbor*, "Summer, Highland Falls" from *Turnstiles*, and "She's Always a Woman" from *The Stranger* each attempt to somehow reconcile the sound and function of the two instruments in the musical setting. Here, he finally succeeds in achieving the long-sought-after delicate balance. The piano anchors the song's harmonic progression, while the acoustic guitar gently supports from above.

Above all, "Through the Long Night" is a near-perfect distillation of the mid-1960s ballad style of the Beatles. In his book, *Tunesmith: In-*

side the Art of Songwriting, Jimmy Webb asserts that the track "sounds so much like Lennon and McCartney circa 1965 that the first time I heard it I was sure that it was a Beatles record I had overlooked. (It has become one of my favorite songs.)"[2] As Webb points out, "Through the Long Night" perfectly captures the acoustic sounds of the Beatles' *Rubber Soul* (1965), but the form of the song seems to be patterned on McCartney's "For No One" from *Revolver* (1966). It should also be noted that in both its mood and its use of tone pedal guitar, the song references "Yes It Is," the B-side to the 1965 single, "Ticket to Ride."

Despite these clever references to various Beatle tracks, the song itself comes out sounding like Billy Joel. From its haunting introduction to its beautiful, distinctive coda, "Through the Long Night" aptly demonstrates how to be influenced by an artist without losing one's own identity in the process.

INTERLUDE: *SONGS IN THE ATTIC* (1981)

While touring to promote *Glass Houses,* a number of recordings were made for possible future use as a Billy Joel live album. During the tour, Joel and his band began to take note of a peculiar energy generated when they played some of his older material. His earlier recordings paled in comparison to those versions being played on tour by his new band. Joel himself described the problem:

> Something was missing on those old records. We liked the songs but the original studio recordings (done mainly with "session players") didn't have nearly as much energy and joy as the live renditions. The live tapes were in fact much closer to the sound I had hoped to capture originally.[3]

According to Dominick Maita, who assisted in the engineering of *Songs in the Attic*, there were different ideas regarding the final format of the album: It could consist entirely of small intimate club settings or large arenas or a combination of the two in the form of a double album.[4] Ultimately, they adapted these ideas to fit within the confines of a single LP. The new album, *Songs in the Attic*, would avoid hits in order to feature live versions of album tracks from Billy Joel's early career. The premise was that a significant number of his fans had just caught up with him and were largely unaware of the work he had been doing prior to *The Stranger*.

The resulting selection of songs is an interesting grab bag from Joel's first four albums: *Turnstiles* fares the best with four tracks featured ("Miami 2017 [Seen the Lights Go Out on Broadway]"; "Summer, Highland Falls"; "Say Goodbye to Hollywood"; and "I've Loved These Days"), followed by *Piano Man* with three ("Captain Jack"; "You're My Home"; and "The Ballad of Billy the Kid"), and two tracks each from *Cold Spring Harbor* ("She's Got a Way" and "Everybody Loves You Now") and *Streetlife Serenade* ("Streetlife Serenader" and "Los Angelenos"). The album is remarkably consistent in quality, and demonstrates that Billy Joel's material had staying power.

THE NYLON CURTAIN (1982)

Overview

Following the tours to promote *Glass Houses* (1980), and the subsequent release of *Songs in the Attic* (1981), Billy Joel decided to take more time with his next project. More than he had ever done before, Joel would now employ the recording studio as a tool in the compositional process. The goal was to create a work that would stand as a unified statement. The resulting album reached back to the exotic instrumental sounds of the late 1960s, in order to comment on American life in the early 1980s. In both his songwriting and his vocal performances for *The Nylon Curtain*, it seemed clear that Joel had been deeply affected by the passing of John Lennon:

> I felt a genuine sadness that John was gone, that there were never going to be any other John Lennon recordings. The Beatles were over; we'd all accepted that. But as much as I had loved them and as easy as it was for me to idolize Paul McCartney, I had never realized how much John Lennon meant to me, how much he and Paul were the irreplaceable sweet and sour. It was only later that I realized I was channeling John in a lot of the vocals on that album.[5]

The album paints a grim portrait of American life toward the end of the twentieth century. Here, Billy Joel revisits the postwar "New World celebrators" and discovers that most of what they had looked forward to in the heady days of the New Frontier has never come to pass. From the various traumatic political assassinations (John F. Kennedy, Martin Luther King, and Robert Kennedy) to the seemingly endless Vietnam War, from oil shortages to unemployment lines, the album channels the disappointment and disillusionment of an entire generation. As he did on *Streetlife Serenade* and *52nd Street*, Joel once again delves into musical texture and color, and both of those are in abundant supply on the opening track.

"Allentown"

In keeping with the effects-driven approach of late '60s record production, the first sound we hear is a piercing factory whistle that signals the opening of "Allentown." The lyrical content defines the dramatic landscape of the entire album. The verses sketch out the lives of workers in an American steel industry town. We quickly learn about their parents who met and married in postwar America and settled down to raise a family. Now, however, the steel factories are closing down and the means supporting those families is disappearing at an alarming rate. In the process, the culture is abandoned as an increasing number of people conclude they have no choice but to pull up stakes and move on.

The steady workman-like rhythmic pattern in the musical setting emulates the clock-like regularity of industrial machines, emphasized through the use of an additional effect—the actual sound of a pile driver. However, the chord progression that moves through this pattern is effectively humanized by the addition of non-chord tones. These coloristic clusters suggest the rich complexity of the lives of the workers who run the factory machines. In the process, they succeed in challenging the dehumanizing logic of a profit-driven society. Billy Joel was very fond of this track, which he described as having "an Aaron Copland–influenced arrangement of major sevenths that's percussive and stirring. Gives me goosebumps it's got so much classic, shoulder-to-the-wheel Americana in it."[6]

"Laura"

The Americana that was evident on "Allentown" is followed by a fascinating track on which Billy Joel revisits the Beatle influence last heard on "Through the Long Night" from *Glass Houses*. However, while that track principally re-created the approach of Beatle Paul McCartney circa *Rubber Soul* and *Revolver*, this time the model is clearly *Sgt. Pepper*–era John Lennon. The lyric describes a situation in which the singer can't seem to shake off the influence of a woman who calls him late at night and relates her personal difficulties. Even though they only seem to connect through long-distance phone calls, she maintains a curious hold on him. Via the telephone line, she is able to push his buttons and manipulate him into a state of frustration and confusion.

The setting of "Laura" creates a driving, heavy rock sound that references the dirge-like musical effects created by the Beatles on "Strawberry Fields Forever" and "I Am the Walrus." Interestingly, the character of Laura, although pitiful and seemingly harmless, may also be potentially dangerous, as demonstrated by her desire to control. In this regard, the music creates an appropriately mysterious atmosphere, sometimes dark and frightening, but always compelling. Here, Joel successfully incorporates Lennonesque musical ideas into his own distinctive approach to pop. In this regard, his only real peer was Jeff Lynne of Electric Light Orchestra, who explored similar effects on songs like "Mister Kingdom" from the album *Eldorado* (1974).

"Allentown" and "Laura" respectively portray different aspects of the cultural distress of the early 1980s. "Allentown" gives listeners an overview of the economic challenges of the era. It also stresses the human implications of these challenges. The human factor is further explored in the title character of "Laura." Her response to the anxieties caused by an unpredictable economy is to cultivate a world of fear-driven fantasy.

At this time, Billy Joel had been facing significant personal challenges of his own. His marriage to Elizabeth Weber was coming to a sad and contentious end. In addition to the personal stress this would cause, she had also been managing his musical career; thus, his business affairs were about to change for the better—and for the worse. As if all this wasn't upsetting enough, during the sessions for *The Nylon Curtain*, Joel was involved in a motorcycle accident in which he suffered serious injuries to his hands.[7] Things had been getting much too dark and dismal, and some good news was desperately needed.

On *The Nylon Curtain,* Joel had employed the complex textures of the late 1960s in order to portray an increasingly complex and confusing modern world. For his next album, he would reach back even further in order to retrieve the more carefree musical era that preceded it.

AN INNOCENT MAN (1983)

Overview

With *An Innocent Man* (1983), Billy Joel offered listeners an album of songs that referenced the great rock and R&B records of the late 1950s and early 1960s. This decidedly upbeat collection works as a tribute—or a pastiche bordering on parody—that emphasizes the importance of the various compositional models employed for each of the tracks. In the process, it reveals Joel's exceptional abilities as composer, performer, and pop musicologist. When compared with his earlier albums, the musical structures of *An Innocent Man* are fairly conventional. However, Joel's brilliance shines through on tracks like "This Night" and "Leave a Tender Moment Alone."

"This Night"

The lyrics describe the mysterious nature of a particular night being shared by a young couple. The two have evidently known each other for a while, but have not yet consummated their relationship. Although initially resistant, the singer begins to woo the woman by telling her that there is something uniquely special about this night. We learn that both are refugees from broken relationships and have had their fair share of heartache and pain. Yet somehow, they've been drawn together into a timeless moment that must be cherished.

The setting of the verse draws heavily on the music of groups like Dion and the Belmonts, the Platters, and the Five Satins. The particular model employed here seems to be "Tears on My Pillow" recorded by Little Anthony and the Imperials in 1958. In keeping with that style, the verse features a repeating I–vi–ii–V chord progression. This pattern tends to generate energy and expectation. In that regard, it sets the stage for the arrival of a remarkable chorus.

The liner notes for *An Innocent Man* list the cowriters of "This Night" as Billy Joel and L. V. Beethoven.[8] This seemingly humorous reference is actually quite accurate, since Joel borrowed the melody of his chorus from the second movement of Beethoven's Piano Sonata No. 8 in C Minor, Op.13 ("Pathétique"). Remarkably, these two melodies fit together beautifully. Here, Joel astutely points to the parallels between classical music and doo-wop in a manner similar to the way in which he drew parallels between classical music and jazz. All in all, "This Night" is an impressive and effective track that would portend developments in Billy Joel's music in the coming decades.

"Leave a Tender Moment Alone"

The penultimate cut from *An Innocent Man* (1983) is one of Joel's most tightly structured and appealing songs. Initially, it sounds more like the 1970s than the early 1960s. However, there seem to be several models at work here, and this blend keeps the song well within the album's overall theme. The first model is arguably Minnie Ripperton's "Lovin' You" (1975), which features a similar descending chord progression in the verse. In addition, Joel seems to reference the harmonic sophistication of "Sweet Blindness" (1968) by Laura Nyro, a brilliant songwriter who drew heavily on the music of the early 1960s for inspiration.

The lyric of "Leave a Tender Moment Alone" describes a delicate pas de deux being played by the singer and his love interest. He takes note of the fact that the two often seem to be "out of sync." For instance, he nervously tries to amuse her with jokes when there really is no need, because she has already accepted him. Thus, in some ways, his strategy only serves to push her further away. She also seems to hold back during the moments when he is at his most relaxed.

The setting is one of the most beautiful that Joel ever produced. It has a timeless quality that seems to touch on multiple musical eras simultaneously. Of particular interest is an exotic chord progression in the bridge that seems largely inspired by jazz. Given the diatonic focus of the pop music of the time, Joel was concerned about how such a gesture might be received by a pop audience. During the album sessions, he asked arranger David Matthews if he thought the chords might be a bit too complex for pop. Matthews gave it a listen and assured him they would be fine.[9]

One of the most remarkable touches on the track is the contribution of Toots Thielemans on chromatic harmonica. Following up on a strategy he had employed on "Night Game" from Paul Simon's *Still Crazy After All These Years* (1975), Phil Ramone invited the jazz legend to play on a Billy Joel session. Said Ramone, "Toots Thielemans was one of my favorite people to utilize, but I'd only use him where I felt it was the most precious moment in the record. He played harmonica different than anybody else."[10]

6

FAMOUS LAST WORDS

With *Glass Houses* (1980), *The Nylon Curtain* (1982), and *An Innocent Man* (1983), Billy Joel had moved progressively deeper into his musical past. In the process, he left little doubt regarding his abilities as a musical craftsman of the first order. His artistry also continued to grow and develop with songs that tackled important social issues. His ability to connect these issues with political and social history reflected his lifelong interest in the subject. This interest would continue to be reflected on songs for upcoming albums.

In the mid-1980s, Billy Joel took a break from his career, and concentrated on home and family. In March 1985, he married Christie Brinkley and in December of that year the couple welcomed a daughter, Alexa Ray. As one might expect, the birth of his first child had a profound effect on Joel:

> When Alexa finally arrived, it was the most joyful moment of my life. We asked a nurse to take a picture, but we didn't know if you were allowed to lift her out of the little bin she was resting in, so the picture is of us holding her like a baby pizza that's just come through the door.[1]

During this period no new albums appeared, but Columbia Records did release *Greatest Hits Volume I & Volume II*, a twenty-six-song compilation that provided new listeners with a serviceable overview of Billy Joel's career to that point. It also featured two new tracks: "You're Only Human (Second Wind)" sits well within the keyboard-driven pop sound of its era. The poignant lyric references Joel's own brush with suicide and urges young people to not lose hope no matter how bleak things may seem. "The Night Is Still Young" reveals a young man struggling with questions concerning the delicate balance between career and family. In the process, he begins to wonder if the two can ever be reconciled at all.

THE BRIDGE (1986)

Overview

On *The Nylon Curtain*, Billy Joel had cast a critical eye on the economic realities of life in the 1980s. With *The Bridge*, he appeared to be surrendering to that era's musical excesses completely. The album's keyboard-driven and reverb-laden sound is certainly consistent with the bonus tracks that were added to *Greatest Hits Volume I & Volume II* (1985). However, as compared with those two tracks, or with any of his albums from the early 1980s, *The Bridge* displays a noticeable lack of inspiration. According to Joel himself, problems plagued the entire project:

> I wasn't simpatico with the musicians, some of whom I'd been working with a long time. I don't think the material was good; I was pressured by management to put it out too fast. By the end, I sort of gave up caring, which for me was unusual. I remember reading bad reviews and agreeing with them.[2]

Nevertheless, *The Bridge* does feature several worthwhile tracks to recommend. Overall, the album constitutes an interesting attempt to retrieve the stylistic eclecticism that Joel was known for in the 1970s. In the spirit of *Turnstiles* and *52nd Street*, the album features an attractive ballad that experiments with jazz pop elements within the context of Joel's ballad style.

"This Is the Time"[3]

The lyrics of this song are largely impressionistic. The main idea concerns the potentiality created by the relationship of a young couple. In

Kurt Vonnegut fashion, the story seems to be resonating forward and backward in time. The singer considers the possibility of family ties that can result from this relationship. He also describes the feeling of warmth that will come from a memory that is being created in the present. In a *Rolling Stone* interview from 1986, Joel described the song's narrative: "That's a strange song, in that part of it is the past, part of it is the present, and part of it is reminiscing about what the future will be."[4]

The musical setting beautifully enhances the intriguing and unusual lyric. The verses employ a pattern of exotic jazz-derived quartal intervals (fourths). These intervals move repeatedly over a circular harmonic progression that features an equally exotic ninth chord. The resulting ambiguity creates a curious, floating quality in the musical setting. The verse then segues abruptly into a march-like chorus section that recalls the valedictory ballad style Joel had previously employed on "Tomorrow Is Today." The stark contrast between these two disparate harmonic and rhythmic elements creates an effective musical symbol for the shifting temporalities of the text.

"Big Man on Mulberry Street"

While writing the songs for *The Bridge* album, Billy Joel rented space in the Puck Building in downtown Manhattan in order to work. Periodically, however, he experienced writer's block and would venture out in search of inspiration. In his interview with Judy Carmichael, Joel talked about what he found:

> I would play all night and if I didn't come up with anything, I would bop down Mulberry Street, down Little Italy to get some food. And I made up this persona, this kind of big city walk. . . . And I became this character, this fictional character. It was all made up in my head. "Yeah, I'm a big man on Mulberry Street." Film noir, you know? I was black and white.[5]

The lyric is consistent with Joel's account of his experiences in Little Italy. It also serves to flesh out the feelings of a character in search of relevance. Like a stage actor who works from the outside in to create a persona, the big man here walks the walk, talks the talk, and tries to act important in order to feel it. As Joel points out, there is a definite cinematic quality to the scene, one that is decidedly film noir, i.e., black and white. Thus, the character may well be related to those everyday people who inhabited the world of *The Stranger*.

The musical setting is a richly active big-band setting that suggests the style of Count Basie. The introduction consists of a dynamic instrumental brass motive that recurs throughout the song. It seems to rhythmically represent the main character's walk down Mulberry Street. The verse that follows this musical motif is more intimate and quiet, suggesting that the scene is taking place at night. Perhaps the character is creeping past alleys where intimacies and feelings can be expressed beyond the hustle and bustle of the main street. There is also a contrasting section that enhances this quality in terms of a meditation by the main character. It explores his deeper feelings in relation to his desire to be more recognized by others. The main brass motive returns in the form of a coda as the character walks off triumphantly into the night.

STORM FRONT (1989)

Overview

While touring to support *The Bridge*, Billy Joel and his entourage performed a series of concerts behind the Iron Curtain. In many ways, this visit to the Soviet Union was indicative of a gradual melting of tensions between East and West and seemed to portend, culturally at least, the subsequent end of the Cold War in 1991. During the tour, Joel met and befriended a young Russian named Viktor. The two had grown up on opposite sides of the Cold War, but discovered that they had a great deal in common. On his next album, Billy Joel would memorialize their friendship and his entire experience in the Soviet Union with the song "Leningrad."[6]

Prior to recording his next album, Joel uncovered some rather severe financial problems that were occurring within his organization. These problems traced back to the years he was being managed by his ex-wife, Elizabeth. After the two divorced in 1982, Joel decided to retain her brother, Frank Weber, as his new manager. Evidently, Weber had been making some questionable investments that had resulted in a drastic reduction of the Joels' personal wealth. As a result, he would have to record and tour extensively in order to pay off the legal bills required to put his financial affairs back in order.[7]

The Bridge (1986) would be the last Billy Joel studio album to be produced by Phil Ramone. For his next album, Joel approached Mick Jones of Foreigner to see if he might be interested in coproducing. Jones was understandably hesitant about stepping into the shoes of Phil Ramone, as he explains:

> It was a little daunting for me in that I knew Phil's successful history with Billy. And I admired him as one of the leading producer-arrangers who'd been there from early on. He'd worked with Sinatra at one point, which was kind of wild. We had a certain mutual respect. And I just remember that afterward we bumped into each other at the Grammys, where I was up for producer [cocredited with Billy] with that album. And [Phil] said, "You know, Mick, if it was anybody else, I'd have been really pissed. But you did a great job, and I'm really very happy—and congratulations." And I thought, *Wow, that's a real gent.*[8]

The album they created was *Storm Front.* Here, Joel revisits some of the harder rock sounds of *Glass Houses* (1980), but with a touch of the R&B that had been a feature of *An Innocent Man.* There is also a good deal of stylistic variety, which connects with the eclectic nature of Joel's albums from the 1970s. *Storm Front* features a number of interesting tracks, such as the late twentieth-century history lesson of "We Didn't Start the Fire," and the exuberant "I Go to Extremes," which blends rock 'n' roll energy with a chord progression typical of a pop ballad. The album concludes with a meditative track titled "And So It Goes," a song that might best be described as a secular hymn.

"We Didn't Start the Fire"

With this lyric, Billy Joel moves in rapid succession through a series of memes and cultural events that characterized the four decades since his birth in 1949, as he himself points out: "The chain of news events and personalities came easily—mostly they just spilled out of my memory as fast as I could scribble them down."[9] His text works as a kind of collage of references that includes significant works of art such as the novels *The Catcher in the Rye* and *Stranger in a Strange Land,* as well as films like *Lawrence of Arabia* and *The King and I*. Collectively, the lyric seems to reveal Joel's cynical attitude regarding the direction of human culture, perhaps best expressed by the line that refers to the assassination of President John F. Kennedy in 1963.

The musical setting of the text is steeped in 1980s production values. These have not aged well, but do provide a nice contrast with the minimal musical materials of the song. Earlier, we asserted that a particular part of the opening section of "Prelude/Angry Young Man" marked the final appearance of the country and western sound on a Billy Joel recording. While this is technically true, according to Billy Joel, the chorus melody of "We Didn't Start the Fire" originated as "Jolie," an unfinished country ballad: "I had a chord progression that originally belonged to a country song I was trying to write, and I sandwiched the words into those chords."[10]

Over time, "We Didn't Start the Fire" has tended to divide listeners. Some have praised the song's historical sweep and assert its importance as a tool for learning. Others find it redundant, severely lacking in melody, and derivative of the allegedly more authentic "It's the End of the World as We Know It" by REM. However one chooses to regard "We Didn't Start the Fire," it must be acknowledged that the song is powerful, and in a live setting works very well indeed.

"I Go to Extremes"

In keeping with the title, the text deals with the polar opposites that exist within the narrator's own personality. He is in the process of trying to explain to his lover that in spite of his best efforts, his nature has caused him to swing wildly between elation and despair. He attempts to navigate effectively through his own emotional fog, but has come to understand that, like the weather, his own temperament can be wildly unpredictable. There is also the sense that he probably wouldn't change things even if he could, because he has become addicted to the emotional highs these sudden shifts can bring.

"I Go to Extremes" features a remarkable musical setting that avoids any overt references to the text. It does, however, reference some of Joel's earliest compositions, specifically "Tomorrow Is Today" and "Everybody Loves You Now," both featured on *Cold Spring Harbor* (1971). All three songs share the same key (C major), as well as similar elements in their respective chord progressions. There is another interesting touch that relates to Billy Joel as a natural musicologist. The chorus makes a subtle motivic reference to the popular standard "Ebb Tide" (1953), written by Robert Maxwell and Carl Sigman. In live performances from the period, Billy Joel made this connection exceedingly clear by slyly modifying his chorus melody so that it became a direct quote from the song.

"And So It Goes"

"I Go to Extremes" finds its companion piece on *Storm Front* with this quietly meditative closing track. The text attempts to deal with the emerging realization that a current relationship cannot last. In the process, the narrator meditates on a fundamental separateness between people that remains no matter how deeply they are drawn together in the moment. At the end of the song, there is a sense of resignation, which suggests a sad acceptance of the inevitable.

The musical setting here seems to reference the chorales of J. S. Bach by way of Randy Newman's ballad "I Think It's Going to Rain Today" (1966). However, Joel puts a unique spin on the material by having the piano consistently employ harsh dissonances in the accompaniment, as he himself points out:

> I did have a strategy for that song—almost every chord had a dissonant note in it, which to me was conveying what's just beneath the words: a kind of pessimism and resignation, because I knew it really wasn't going to work out.[11]

The use of dissonance references a jazz practice in which extended harmonies such as sevenths, ninths, and thirteenths can be compressed together within the chord voicing in a decidedly dissonant manner. Thus, "And So It Goes" can be seen as a synthesis between the two genres (jazz and classical) that Joel had so often attempted to reconcile in the past.

RIVER OF DREAMS (1993)

Overview

Storm Front (1989) had featured two songs with intriguing ideas that seemed to indicate that Billy Joel was still very interested in the creation of instrumental music. In the aforementioned ballad "Leningrad," along with the driving pop anthem "State of Grace," the complex melodic introductions suggested that Joel was eager to move in new compositional directions. For the most part, however, these directions would have to wait. He still had one more song cycle to complete.

For his next album, *River of Dreams* (1993), Joel changed producers yet again. On the advice of Don Henley, he enlisted the help of Danny Kortchmar, a well-known L.A. guitarist and composer. Initial exploratory sessions with Joel's own band had taken place in a makeshift studio on Shelter Island, New York. Kortchmar, however, was determined to get Billy out of his comfort zone. He preferred to use studio pros, and also wanted to work in a top-notch studio in New York City. The resulting collection of songs was rather conventional. However, three tracks in particular stand out from the rest.[12]

"The Great Wall of China"

"The Great Wall of China" expresses Billy Joel's deep feelings of resentment regarding the actions of his former manager, Frank Weber. As previously noted, Weber was the brother of Joel's ex-wife and had taken over the management of Joel's organization following the singer's divorce from Elizabeth Weber. These events are referenced in the relatively straightforward verses. However, the choruses are decidedly metaphorical in their use of the Great Wall as a symbol of the achievements that Joel and Weber could have reached were it not for his personal betrayal. In addition, the wall stands as a symbol of the permanent barrier that now exists between the two men.

The lyric also contains an interesting element that connects with Billy Joel's use of cinematic techniques on *The Stranger* and *52nd Street*. In an iteration of the song's chorus, he offers a variation on a segment of dialogue from the film *On the Waterfront* (1954). In that film, during a scene in which Terry Malloy (Marlon Brando) confronts his brother Charley (Rod Steiger) about the mismanagement of his boxing career, the following dialogue is heard:

Terry: You was my brother, Charley. You shoulda looked out for me a little bit. You shoulda taken care of me just a little bit, so I wouldn't have to take them dives for the short-end money.

Charley: I had some bets down for you. You saw some money.

Terry: You don't understand, I coulda had class! I coulda been a contender. I coulda been somebody, instead of a bum, which is what I am. Let's face it. It was you, Charley.[13]

In Joel's version, he cleverly repurposes this scene's dialogue so that the person being addressed throughout the lyric is now the one who missed his chance.

The musical setting of the verse evokes the rhythmic drive and sputtering vocal delivery of the Rolling Stones. In contrast, the chorus revisits the colorful Beatlesque sounds that Joel last explored on *The Nylon Curtain* (1982). The use of these contrasting elements accesses the perceived rivalry between the Beatles and the Rolling Stones, and thus underscores the combative stance of the lyric. The orchestrations by Ira Newborn greatly enhance the song's Beatlesque qualities. His countermelodies add a sense of urgency to an already compelling track.

"Lullaby (Goodnight, My Angel)"

The lyric tells the story of a father putting his young child to bed. Before falling asleep, the child asks him what happens when we die. The father responds with a brief description of human lives touching one another beyond the limits of mortality. He says that our actions, born of love, live long beyond the time we each spend here on earth. He reminds the child of the times they have shared together and how important these remain to him. Someday, she will grow up and have children of her own, and these memories will fill her heart as well as the lullaby she will sing to send them off to sleep.

The setting for this remarkable text is one of the most beautiful that Joel ever produced. The chords and melody caress the lyric without once getting in the way of the meaning. The orchestration by composer

Ira Newborn finds the timbral subtlety and nuance that Billy Joel had been reaching for as far back as *Streetlife Serenade* (1974). Newborn's sensitivity to the underlying composition is evident in his comments for the documentary *Billy Joel: Shades of Grey* (1993):

> It's a lullaby, and I thought about having a big string section, but the more I listened to it, I realized that it was intimate, and he was singing it in an intimate fashion, and it was a very simple piano part. So, I realized the only thing to do is have basically a small group type of thing, like a string quartet and some French horns, 'cause that's a nice warm sound, and generally speaking, most people don't have symphony orchestras in their bedrooms.[14]

"Lullaby (Goodnight, My Angel)" creates a seamless blend of melody and text, and leaves little doubt as to Billy Joel's mastery of song form. The track also explores pure music through its powerfully effective instrumental bridge and its richly colored orchestration. Joel had already succeeded in integrating jazz and pop elements within "And So It Goes" from *Storm Front* (1989). Here, he blends pop and classical in a manner that suggests the completion of a long and prolific musical arc.

"The River of Dreams"

At the conclusion of chapter 4, we explored Paul Simon's use of chromatic elements derived from jazz process as a way of expanding his compositional style. As described by Walter Everett, "Simon's chromatic music from the mid to late 1970s constitutes a kind of midpoint in an arch that stretches from the diatonic music of the Simon and Garfunkel years to the diatonicism of Simon's more recent music."[15] With the release of *Graceland* in 1986, Paul Simon had fully returned to the more elemental diatonic chord structures of folk and early rock 'n' roll. Billy Joel would also initiate a return of sorts with the centerpiece of his last album of pop music. With "The River of Dreams," he echoed Simon's journey, and also revisited the doo-wop traditions of his own youth.

The lyrics describe a personal voyage taken in order to find spiritual fulfillment and some kind of answer to the problems of relationship and self. Essentially, the singer is seeking redemption and renewal. He talks about the human desire to return to the river that connects us with the ocean that is our original source. In that sense, the lyric echoes remarks made in 1962 by President John F. Kennedy:

> I really don't know why it is that all of us are so committed to the sea, except I think it is because . . . we all came from the sea. And it is an interesting biological fact that all of us have, in our veins the exact same percentage of salt in our blood that exists in the ocean, and, therefore, we have salt in our blood, in our sweat, in our tears. We are tied to the ocean. And when we go back to the sea, whether it is to sail or to watch it we are going back from whence we came.[16]

The musical setting of the track is based around a repeating ostinato riff, played by Joel on piano and by Danny Kortchmar on rhythm guitar. The chords of this riff are diatonic and provide the foundation for what is arguably the most compelling and organic groove in Billy Joel's entire catalog. This kind of chordal pattern is difficult to sustain on piano, but the easy strumming of the electric guitar provides wonderful support. It creates an effective counterpoint to the reconciliation between piano and acoustic guitar that was achieved on "Through the Long Night" from *Glass Houses* (1980).

The coda provides a lovely gesture that connects with *An Innocent Man*, as well as the early musical inspirations of Paul Simon. As the aforementioned riff continues to play at the end of the track, Billy Joel begins to sing the opening lines of the doo-wop classic "Gloria." Written by Leon René, "Gloria" was originally recorded in 1946 by Bob Hayward with the Buddy Baker Orchestra, and then again by the Mills Brothers in 1948. At the end of "The River of Dreams," Billy Joel quotes from the subsequent and arguably definitive interpretation of "Gloria" recorded by the Cadillacs in 1954.[17] Ever the pop musicologist, he manages here to connect the underlying progression of his song with a 1950s classic, written in a style of music that was an inspiration to Paul Simon, as well as the streetlife serenaders of Joel's own youth.

7

FANTASIES, CONCLUSIONS, AND THE GIRL AT THE PARTY

As a composer, Billy Joel has always tended toward a kind of musical alchemy. He has a unique talent that enables him to move easily through a variety of genres, for example, pop, jazz, classical, folk, rock, blues, country and western, and more. In his recorded works, he has consistently attempted to weave these seemingly discrete influences into a tapestry of sound and style.

Cold Spring Harbor (1971) was an ambitious album that revealed Billy Joel's youthful aspirations as an artist. It was an audacious way to begin a solo career, that is, with a concept album chronicling the passage from adolescence into young adulthood. Given the limited resources that he had at his disposal, it's understandable that he really wasn't able to pull the whole thing off in a manner the material deserves. Nevertheless, it's an impressive effort in which Joel plants a number of musical seeds that will blossom on subsequent albums, most notably *Piano Man* (1973), on which he first began to find his voice as a songwriter.

Streetlife Serenade (1974) was an intriguing experiment on which Joel sought a context for the kind of isolated vignettes that were found on *Piano Man* (1973). The album offered listeners a painterly view of mid-'70s America that connected with the work of Edward Hopper. As he had done on *Piano Man*, Joel continued to sketch his characters in broad strokes, but the arrangements here are far more varied and interesting. Joel and producer Michael Stewart pared down the instrumentation and created subtle timbral effects that attempted to bring the "streetlife" world into focus. In the process, the lives of the various characters resonate with what might be described as vivid emotional color.

Streetlife Serenade certainly has its moments of brilliance, but overall, it seems strangely incomplete. Perhaps we can assert that the expanded approach to musical color makes the album sound much better than it is. Concerning the streetlife concept, Joel seemed to have a lot to say, but at this point, may have lacked the artistic maturity to say it. After all, although this was his third complete album, he was still only twenty-five years old! As we'll soon see, he will revisit these themes and develop them much further on his next three collections.

With *Turnstiles* (1976), Billy Joel was sitting pretty. He had validated his own artistic instincts by recording the album with his own band rather than with a group of studio musicians. As a songwriter, he had grown in ways scarcely imaginable just a few years earlier. Within its eclectic and impressive sequence of songs, *Turnstiles* also features "Prelude/Angry Young Man," a track that works as a hybrid (pop anthem/ extended form) within a hybrid (folk song/pop anthem) within a larger hybrid (classical/jazz). The listener could perhaps regard this track as a stylistic exercise that buys Joel the time he needs to create his next experiment with extended form, "Scenes from an Italian Restaurant."

The Stranger (1977) can be considered in terms of the way the various characters who populate the album are evoked as living, breathing human beings. The production strategy implicitly asserts the need to push the limits of a variety of art forms (popular music, cinema, and sound recording) in order to better understand the human condition. Like the characters of *The Stranger*, we all have needs, wants, and desires, but we only show others the face we want them to see. Through the blending of cinematic technique, record production, and compositional form, Billy Joel and producer Phil Ramone created a portal into the world of human experience. In the process, they gave listeners the means to explore that world and find their own humanity in the lives of the characters who live there.

Billy Joel had now arrived on his own terms. He had stuck to his guns, followed his artistic instincts, and saw those instincts validated by the widespread acceptance of his work. Through his collaboration with Phil Ramone, he had advanced to a new artistic level through the creation of an effective and innovative framework for his wide-ranging musical ideas. The integration of cinematic techniques into the production process for *The Stranger* was, in retrospect, a masterstroke. It allowed him to develop his distinctive musical vision to new heights of creative expression.

52nd Street (1978) was a successful follow-up that continued to explore the many cinematic tropes of *The Stranger*, this time in living color. As on the previous album, the characters here are consumed with the challenging realities of daily life. Just as he had originally tried to do on the move from *Piano Man* (1973) to *Streetlife Serenade* (1974), Joel enhances and dignifies these characters through an increasingly expansive palette of musical color. The stylistic means of this expansion was the continued integration of the jazz threads that were a prominent feature on *Turnstiles* (1976). In a sense, jazz music is used here to "score" the lives of the various characters. Thus, it becomes a testament to human dignity and the creative power of human expression.

Between 1980 and 1983, Billy Joel released three new studio albums of original material: *Glass Houses*, *The Nylon Curtain*, and *An Innocent Man*. On each of these, he moved deeper into his musical past, exploring a variety of styles with the consummate skills of a master craftsman. On *Glass Houses*, within the guise of a hard-edged sound inspired by punk, he subtly revealed the main influence of the newly energized musical landscape—the Beatles. On *The Nylon Curtain*, Joel retrieved the exotic instrumental textures of the late 1960s as a means of commenting on American life in the early 1980s. For his next album, *An Innocent Man*, he would reach back even further to retrieve the more carefree musical era of the late 1950s and early 1960s.

Writing about *The Beatles* (1968; also known as *The White Album*), scholar Ian MacDonald described "a secret unease in this music, betraying the turmoil beneath the group's business-as-usual facade. Shadows lengthen over the album as it progresses: the slow afternoon of the Beatles' career."[1] In a similar way, shadows lengthen over the latter part of Billy Joel's musical career. Between 1986 and 1993, he released three more albums of new material: *The Bridge*, *Storm Front*, and *River of Dreams*. In retrospect, these work as a kind of muted coda to his career as a composer of popular songs.

The Bridge (1986) attempts to retrieve the eclecticism that was a hallmark of Joel's work in the 1970s. Although it often succeeds in this regard, more often than not the songs seem uninspired. With *Storm Front* (1989), Billy Joel regrouped and created a dynamic collection that revisited the R&B approach of *An Innocent Man*. Interesting ideas are explored here, but a creative fatigue was becoming more and more apparent. On *River of Dreams*, Joel wraps up his career in pop music with an album that worked well as a song cycle and also foregrounded his desire to move toward instrumental music as his primary focus.

FANTASIES & DELUSIONS (2001)

Overview

In the years following the release of *River of Dreams*, Billy Joel made no plans to record another pop album. Eventually, he admitted that he had basically lost interest in the genre and would thereafter be devoting himself to the composition of classical music. In 2001, he emerged from creative hibernation with a new album, *Fantasies & Delusions*. Essentially, this was a collection of new works for solo piano composed in the manner of Chopin, Brahms, Beethoven, and Debussy. Since the pieces were beyond Billy Joel's technical abilities on the instrument, he enlisted the help of Richard Joo, a pianist who had been recommended by Joel's half brother, Alexander.[2]

From the standpoint of the classical music tradition, *Fantasies & Delusions* is an interesting hodgepodge. Essentially, it comes across as a melding of Chopin with Brahms with Debussy, and all of it being filtered through the prism of a Beethoven sonata. Thus, the general consensus is that the album is interesting, but not truly a part of the classical tradition. Nevertheless, it should be pointed out that the listener is often struck by a chord sequence, or a turn of musical phrase, that is quite ingenious and very characteristic of Joel's unique compositional style.

Fantasies & Delusions is arguably more important for what it tells us about the structural integrity of Billy Joel's songs than for any lasting value it may have as classical music. The directed tonal motion toward structural goals that is a primary feature of classical music is also recognizable as an important aspect of his songwriting. A detailed analysis of his musical settings reveals that the vast majority would tend to work well as stand-alone pieces of music, as the composer himself points out: "I was always writing classical music, even the popular songs I wrote. I recognize a lot of them as being classical piano pieces, and that's how I started composing when I was a kid."[3]

In the final analysis, *Fantasies and Delusions* may properly be regarded as an appropriate end note to a brilliant musical career. The twelve albums that Billy Joel recorded and released between 1971 and 1993 had already established a complete body of work. They stand up well when measured against the catalog of the Beatles as a complete artistic statement on the development of popular music. Throughout, Joel explores different possibilities with regard to songwriting, record production, arrangements, and so on. He also made remarkable strides with regard to stylistic connections between seemingly discrete musical genres.

So then, what was the point of all this musical blending? Why even bother? In order to try to answer that question, let's return to my encounter with Victoria, the pianist on the PATH train, in 1978. . . .

"Billy Joel—I don't like him," she said.

"You don't like him?" I replied.

"No, not at all," she said.

"Why not? I mean, why don't you like him?" I struggled.

"Well, I suppose he's a decent musician. He seems to play the piano well enough, but why does he use all those oddly dissonant cluster chords? They don't seem necessary at all. In fact, they just slow things down."

Victoria was referring here to the jazz-derived harmonies that Joel blended with his more classically driven compositional forms.

"Also, I have a real problem with his lyrics," she continued.

"His lyrics? What's wrong with his lyrics?" I stammered.

"Well, he's always telling you what you should be doing in your life. He always seems to want to give you advice on what you need to change in order to be happy," she said.

I tried to get a handle on what Victoria was saying. As she spoke, I raced back through various Billy Joel song lyrics to try to find examples. His albums featured a good number of songs that tended to create vivid character sketches, but I began to see what it was she was getting at. Joel would sometimes use those characters as the springboard for mak-

ing recommendations to his listeners. It never bothered me before, but I could see what she meant.

She continued, "It's not that big a deal, because it's only pop music, right? But, I really don't need someone to tell me what to do. I mean, how does he know what I need?"

She seemed so sure of herself. I didn't know what else to say. At that point, I'd never heard a discouraging word about the man or his music. Following another lengthy and awkward pause, Victoria asked, "So then, what do you like about Billy Joel?"

The remainder of the PATH train ride was quiet. Victoria and I tried to make polite conversation, but truthfully, I wasn't really paying attention. I kept looking at the tunnel lights moving quickly past the window and reassessing my fascination with the music of Billy Joel. We both got off the train at Journal Square and said our goodbyes. "Maybe, I'll see you around," she said, but we both knew that probably wouldn't happen. As I rode the No. 10 bus back to Bayonne, I thought again about what she'd been saying.

A few weeks later, I was talking with my friend Dominick Maita and told him about the incident. I described Victoria's complaint that Joel's lyrics were always telling listeners what to do. Dom thought that this was interesting since, like me, he had yet to encounter anyone with such a strong dislike for Billy Joel or his music. However, he pointed out that many people like to be told what to do, because they have not yet found a way to be creatively self-directed in their own lives. Others, like Victoria, had already found that sense of direction and tended to take unsolicited advice as an invasion of their space.

However, there was something else that kept bothering me about the incident. When we first met, I assumed that Victoria and I would be able to relate and talk to each other as musicians, but this was not the case. In fact, it was as if she and I were speaking completely different languages. I remembered that the jazz improvisation class, the one that I'd left early to attend the Billy Joel concert, was an elective, and was scheduled for late afternoon, long after the conservatory-trained faculty had left for the day.

Years later, I attended graduate school and was impressed by the fact that jazz had become a fully recognized part of the music curriculum. Nevertheless, I soon discovered the same problem I'd encountered with Victoria. In the music theory classes that I taught, there was a language barrier between jazz practitioners and those who studied classical music performance. In class discussions, these students were often talking about the same musical ideas. However, they struggled to understand one another because they were still using different musical languages.

Interestingly enough, I did run into Victoria again. It was eleven years later, at a party on the Upper West Side of Manhattan. The host was a friend of a friend who had just purchased a Steinway grand piano and had hired me to show off the new instrument for his guests. Of course, I spent the entire gig reading out of *The Real Book*, the jazz musician's best friend.

I actually enjoyed these kinds of gigs, because, as was pointed out earlier about "Piano Man," they allow you to remain detached from a situation while still retaining a measure of control. For instance, if a child would ever get fidgety or cross, you could always cheer them up with a chorus of "This Old Man," which was the theme to *Barney the Dinosaur*. For some reason, they also tended to be fascinated by the music from the game show *Jeopardy*, which I liked to play in the piano's upper register.

You could also engage in a certain amount of mischief from this position. In the 1990s, while playing in a local restaurant, I overheard a woman trashing the work of musician Kurt Cobain, who had recently died. "I heard those records," she said. "That's not real music." I immediately began to play the melody of "Heart Shaped Box," one of Cobain's most beautiful and haunting melodies, as a meditative piano solo. The woman then turned to me and said, "Oh, that's lovely. Is it Chopin?" "No," I replied, "Nirvana."

At any rate, this particular party was going relatively smoothly when I noticed an attractive woman seated alone on the sofa. She had brown hair, beautiful green eyes, and was wearing a dark beret that was now out of fashion, but still quite fetching. Then, I suddenly realized—this was Victoria. As I continued to play, I kept looking across at her trying to confirm my recognition. She soon caught one of my glances and got up to come over to the piano.

"Hi, Victoria," I said. "Do you remember me?"

She seemed a bit perplexed. She looked briefly at the tune I was playing from *The Real Book*, and then again at my face, and paused. . . .

"You!" she exclaimed.

"Yes, it's me—the chord player," I said sardonically.

"Ah, don't cultivate that," she said.

"I am well rebuked," I replied.

She sat down next to me on the piano bench and we began to talk. I learned that she had just moved to New York and was now living downtown in the West Village. She had gone on to become a concertizing pianist but had recently given up performing for an academic position that would provide her with some measure of security. She was also recovering from what I gathered was a rather difficult divorce. I then asked her if she remembered our conversation about Billy Joel.

She laughed and said that she did in fact remember it. She also added that she had always felt bad about it, and thought that she'd been a bit too harsh in her assessment of Joel's music. I assured her that it was okay and that, in fact, our conversation had actually been something of a turning point for me. As we spoke, I continued to play. After a little while, she asked what I was playing.

"It's called 'And So It Goes,'" I said.

"Who wrote it?" she asked.

I paused for a moment and then said, "This is by Billy Joel."

"Ah!" she screamed, "You got me!"

She laughed and smacked me across the shoulder. I continued playing. She said she liked the voice leading as well as the overall structure of the piece, which was rather "classical." I added that I also liked the dissonance in the chordal accompaniment that seemed to reference twentieth-century atonal techniques as well as jazz. Victoria agreed. "Oh, and by the way," I added, "the lyrics don't try to offer any advice." She laughed.

So, there you have it. Billy Joel had reached across musical boundaries and enabled Victoria and I to speak and hear one another in a warm and effective manner. Simply stated, his work had helped to bring people together . . .

And isn't that what music is all about?

APPENDIX A

Interview with Ira Newborn
November 20, 2013

Thom: Hi, Ira. So, this book I'm preparing is intended as an exploration of Billy Joel's career as a musician and composer. At this point, I'm still messing around with chapter titles.

Ira: Streetlife Serenaders?

Thom: Possibly. Anyway, I don't think we need to spend a lot of time on biographical material that is available elsewhere. Instead, I'd like to focus on the cultural ground from which Billy emerged as a musician. I remember that you were telling me about your experience of singing with him in the shopping malls.

Ira: The streetlife serenaders?

Thom: Yes.

Ira: Mid-Island Plaza?

Thom: I think so. I remember you mentioning the reverberance of certain buildings near where you grew up.

Ira: Yes, well that's a standard doo-wop thing. Kenny Vance, who was one of the original Jay & the Americans, wrote a tune called "Looking for an Echo," which was exactly what we were doing—looking for any place with reverb such as subways, alleyways, or store entrances where there was glass on either side, and it was good. And lo, it was good [*laughs*]. At the time, we used to sing with three or four different people. The most we ever had at one time was five. And we used to sing songs like, "The Way You Do the Things You Do" in harmony, and "Ooo Baby Baby" by Smokey Robinson. We also sang "The Cheater" by Bob Kuban and The In Men.

Thom: Great tune.

Ira: It was fun. I'll never forget that. And it was the first time that I ever had a real feeling of MUSIC with a bunch of other people. And it was like, "Wow, this is unbelievable."

Thom: Were you studying jazz at that point, or were you mainly playing pop?

Ira: I studied classic [classical] guitar, is that right? Well, I originally started fiddling around on guitar because my grandmother played. When she came to America, she studied guitar at the Third Street Music School Settlement. And since she was studying, her guitar would always be leaning in the corner, so I used to try to play it. Later on, I nagged my mother, and she took me to see a performance by the guitarist Carlos Montoya, and I said, "I want to do THAT!" So, she looked around and found this guy named Lenny Frank near Billy's house. He was an ex-junkie, and he knew Charlie Parker, and he was, like, "out there." Some of the things he taught me still put me ahead of the crowd, but sometimes, it seemed like he didn't know which end was up. But what he did teach me was very good. So, I started taking guitar lessons and he [Lenny Frank] played jazz and he did club dates. I was listening to rock 'n' roll and started trying to play it. It was simple, and this is where I got my ear training. I had a band and there was no sheet music available for rock 'n' roll tunes, so I was the one who was elected to sit next to my record player and write it all down. After a while, I'd say to myself, "Didn't I just hear these chords?" And in the process, I learned that there was something called a [chord] progression that could be reused as long as you changed the melody each time. In retrospect, I was getting an ear-training lesson in harmony, rhythm, and, to an extent, melody. I was still taking guitar lessons with Lenny Frank, but then, for some reason, I stopped, and began taking classical guitar lessons from Miroslav Jessic.

Thom: Did you do this to improve your technique?

Ira: Who knows why? I did that for a while until the teacher passed away from a brain tumor. So, I went back to Lenny [Frank] and was doing pretty good. I was playing music with guys who were way older than me. I was the youngest one in the band. And somewhere around that time, I met Billy who was a good musician and had a similar training to mine. He also had a great sense of humor—and still does.

Thom: So, how did your friendship with Billy begin?

Ira: Ruth Hilfer, his mother's cousin, kept telling my mother, "Oh, Rita. We've got to get Ira and Billy together. They're so talented, blah, blah, blah, blah, blah," lots of stuff along with that. So one day in 1964, I called him up, or my mother called him up, and I went over to his house on 30th and Ervin. The screen door almost came off in my hand because the top hinge wasn't attached. So, I opened the door and this white dog comes up to me, barking incessantly. It turns out that this dog, whose name was Whitey, was deaf! So, he just kept barking. Anyway, that's what they told me. And so Billy and I met and then played some music together in this little room with an upright piano in it.

Thom: A white upright?

Ira: Yeah, it was painted and it had cigarette burns all over it. It looked like something you should throw out. Anyway, when I met with him, I brought *Fake Book No. 1*.

Thom: *The Real Book*?

Ira: No, not *The Real Book*, the first *Fake Book*. It cost thirty-five dollars, and is still illegal, I think. In the process, I found out something interesting. If you look at *Fake Book No. 1*, the tunes are printed very small because they were written on file cards. Then, they would put three of them on a page. Years later, when I came to school here [NYU], I studied with a guy named Frederick Picket, who was a music theory teacher from Vienna. I later found out that he'd once owned a company called Tune-Dex, and he was the one that had put all those tunes on index cards. He literally wrote them all out by hand, and then somebody else put them into the *Fake Book*. He was also an accomplished organist, yet there he was writing out pop tunes at Tunedex. [*Laughs*]

Thom: Wow.

Ira: So anyway, I'm there with Billy. I've brought the *Fake Book* and placed it on the piano. He begins to play from the book, and I'm playing guitar—this crappy guitar. Once, when he left the room to get something, I would sit down at the piano and pick out a tune. It was then that I noticed that a lot of the hammers were broken. When Billy was playing, you couldn't hear that they were broken. He just took note of which keys wouldn't play and then avoided them. I was fourteen or fifteen at the time and I thought that this was impressive. He also played me songs that he'd written, which was also impressive because they were really good. I'd never heard anyone that age composing and playing that well. In fact, I have a tape somewhere of him and I playing one of these original songs in my living room. It was called "Room 12"—a Paul McCartney kind of thing, as I recall. I think it may be on a recent album that contained a lot of old stuff that was never released.

Thom: As a singer, does Billy have perfect pitch?

Ira: Let me put it this way. He doesn't have *real* perfect pitch. He always called it "piano pitch." He knows the sound and timbre of the piano. I have the same thing on the guitar.

Thom: With regard to Billy's songwriting, you mentioned Paul McCartney. At that time, was he writing with an awareness of Paul McCartney?

Ira: He was writing with awareness of Paul McCartney, and also of Elton John.

Thom: Elton seems such an eccentric writer—I mean that as a compliment—whereas Billy seems much more structured in his approach.

Ira: True, but that's what appeals to him. First of all, we used to play all the popular standards. He knew them because of his mother. I knew them too because my mother played everything from Mahalia Jackson to James Brown to Stan Kenton. You name it; I heard it. So, I was able to break them down and recognize the reasons why a certain record sounded a certain way. Billy did the same. He listened and he paid attention. He knows all of those classic tunes. He and I were always talking about writing something like Gilbert & Sullivan, but it never happened.

Thom: If you start with *Cold Spring Harbor* [1971] and end with *The Stranger* [1977], you have five albums that seem to form the foundation of his catalog. By comparison, the albums that followed tend more toward specific themes, for example, *The Nylon Curtain, An Innocent Man*, et cetera. Each contains good material, but they don't seem to have the sense of direction evident in his early work.

Ira: Well, composers, like physicists, tend to start off strong and then taper off.

Thom: The qualities that define us at the outset become mannerisms that later can get in the way.

Ira: Yes, and there are two other things to remember: 1) It's a business, and no one wants to upset the apple cart, and 2) the powers that be know that no artist can crank out album after album without a drop in quality, so they tend to discourage creativity. Even the Beatles had a percentage of songs that didn't make the cut. However, because there were three writers in that band, they could pick and choose. They, of course, were an influence on all of us. I do remember at one point when Billy was having problems with his record company.

Thom: Artie Ripp and Family Productions? Paramount?

Ira: No, Columbia, I think. You've heard of this kind of thing—fights between artists and record companies. But, we all know that artists can be lacking, and record companies can be lacking, too. The artists don't know anything about business, and the companies don't know much about music. Plus, they tend to think that the artists are crazy! Anyway, as I said before, composers, like physicists, tend to start off strong and then taper off.

Thom: Recently, you had mentioned George Martin, someone who helped develop artists, and is part of that tradition that tried to help the artist grow.

Ira: Quincy Jones is another one. When he was at Mercury Records, he was working with Lesley Gore.

Thom: He worked with Lesley Gore? The scope of her classic recordings is amazing.

Ira: That's Quincy.

Thom: Since you had mentioned Carole King, I was also thinking of . . .

Ira: Neil Diamond?

Thom: He's brilliant! And I often think that Billy had the talent to be that kind of artist—a Brill Building songwriter. Unfortunately, by the time he came along, that tradition was in decline.

Ira: Yes, and he was more interested in composing than performing.

Thom: Right. There is also that sense that Joel had similar potential to people like Quincy Jones and Burt Bacharach. The idea that one starts with the song, moves to the arrangement, and then finishes with the production of the recording. One wonders if perhaps he could have gone there. . . .

Ira: He could go there. I remember when I would listen to his songs and I would say, "Wow, this guy is a *real* songwriter." I mean, the power of the material would just jump right out at you.

Thom: The way that "She's Always a Woman," for instance, plays to the final tonic harmony. The whole piece seems to aim for that arrival point. Beautiful.

Ira: He's a songwriter and he's very musical, but he doesn't really think like an arranger, although he is very demanding regarding the various instrumental parts.

Thom: I remember seeing a clip from the *River of Dreams* sessions where he and the producer were trying to work out the arrangement of "Blonde over Blue," and he did seem to have a very clear idea of how it should sound. Perhaps, it's the lingering tradition of keeping the talent in front of the microphone and away from the other side of things. I've often thought that he had the potential for more—if not arranging, then perhaps production.

Ira: I agree. I'd have to say that he is probably the most talented person I've ever met. I mean, I've met John Coltrane, but in terms of songwriting and singing, and a basic musicality, Billy would be the one. He was always reaching for something higher, something better. He didn't have it easy when he was a kid, and I think that really drove him.

Thom: That sensibility seems to come through in the lyrics he writes. And by the way, the high quality of his lyrics is rarely ever mentioned in critiques of his work. I've always been impressed by his ability to paint his melodies with beautiful text.

Ira: Yes, well he's a very intelligent guy.

Thom: Could you talk more about your musical experiences with Joel?

Ira: Sure. As I said before, we used to play together a lot, so we learned a lot together. A few years later, I remember hanging out at his place in Oyster Bay. That's where I taught him how to modulate, by the way. You can hear it on *Cold Spring Harbor*.

Thom: From what you've said, it seems like he has relied on you for grounding.

Ira: Maybe. But, I don't think he likes it when I disagree with him [*laughs*]. Also, going back to what I said earlier, he didn't have an easy time growing up, and I think that at an early age it really sunk in that most people had more than he did.

Thom: Critics have commented on the pessimistic thread running through his lyrics.

Ira: Well, sad songs say so much. And by the way, I was always annoyed when critics would knock Billy in their reviews. This one guy would go out of his way to say that Billy wasn't really rock 'n' roll, and that he was derivative of Elton John, who was so much better—so what. He would keep saying this in review after review. Hey, I got your point, let it go.

Thom: I first heard Billy in 1973 with the "Piano Man" single. I didn't hear the full album until a few years later. Many critics claim that the *Piano Man* album was patterned on Elton's *Tumbleweed Connection*, but I don't really hear it.

Ira: I don't think that's true. Even though some of it may sound derivative, that doesn't mean all of it sounds derivative. And frankly, to me *Piano Man* sounds like Billy. Along those same lines, consider a song like "The Longest Time." A critic might say that it sounds derivative, but to me it's authentic doo-wop. The trick is to take an influence and turn it into something that is clearly your own. "I'm Down" may be influenced by Little Richard, but it still sounds like the Beatles. It all depends on how you do it. Mediocre composers borrow; great composers steal.

Thom: Another example that comes to mind is "Roberta" from *Streetlife Serenade* [1974]. The introduction, which uses a pattern of sixths, seems to be a retrograde of the introduction to Neil Diamond's "I Am, I Said."

Ira: Well, you can't get arrested for using sixths. They're basic musical elements, and thus can't be copyrighted. They're fair game. But, if you use them, it's going to sound similar to all the other works that ever used them.

Thom: By the way, the cut time in "Roberta" drives me crazy. There's something about the roll of that groove and the way the melody syncopates across the top that is just so intricate. It's perfect! And maybe that kind of thing is what causes some critics to complain. It's as if they want his stuff to sound spontaneous as opposed to carefully worked out.

Ira: The trouble with critics is that they claimed that Billy wasn't really rock 'n' roll. And you know, he's not! He has a variety of diverse influences that he blends into a unique sound. Rock 'n' roll is one of those influences. But if he comes up with a chord that isn't technically a rock 'n' roll chord he says, so what, I'm gonna use it anyway.

Thom: Do you think he lost something by playing in big arenas? In the early part of his career, he seemed right at home in clubs and theaters.

Ira: I think that any performer—and Billy is definitely a performer, and a good one—would be reluctant to pass up the opportunity to play big arenas. It probably seemed like an interesting challenge.

Thom: Around that time, he released *52nd Street* [1978]. I find that album to be particularly interesting in terms of the jazz elements that he brings to it.

Ira: I agree.

Thom: He seemed to be pushing the envelope in a way that seems consistent with the late 1970s work of Joni Mitchell and Steely Dan. It sounds as if he wants to expand the language of pop and rock by using a more sophisticated harmony derived from jazz. "Rosalinda's Eyes" has an amazing instrumental section that sounds influenced by Bob James, but the song is tucked away on side two of the album!

Ira: Because, it's not commercial.

Thom: Right, but it's so good!

Ira: Look, when the record company hears that you can write hits— as Billy can—then that's what they want you to do. You can include other kinds of tunes too, as long as you have a hit that will sell the album. It's business.

Thom: You're right.

Ira: Personally, I'm not a fan of business, but it's reality.

Thom: I understand. It just seems to me that there's so much there that is underappreciated in his work. His practice of writing entire albums suggests that he was conceiving of his albums as song cycles. This could have been cultivated by his record label, but wasn't.

Ira: That's not what they do anymore. It's sad, but true.

Thom: Given that, I think those albums from the early to mid-'70s are even more impressive when you consider that he did so much of the conceptual work on his own.

Ira: I agree. I saw a lot of that happening, and I still have great faith in him and his talent.

Thom: Oh, well. It's only music. Right?

Ira: Yes, but not to us.

Thom: Thank you for taking the time to talk with me, Ira.
Ira: You're welcome.

APPENDIX B

Interview with Rhys Clark
June 9, 2014

Thom: Hi, Rhys.

Rhys: Hey, Thom.

Thom: Thank you very much for taking the time to talk with me today.

Rhys: You're very welcome.

Thom: First of all, how did you get started in music?

Rhys: Well, at the age of five, the primary school I attended had sessions called "Music Appreciation." The teacher would bring out various instruments, and one of the instruments happened to be a snare drum. Out of all the instruments, this particular snare drum struck me as being "the real thing," as opposed to say, a toy xylophone [*laughs*]. All of the instruments seemed like toys to me except the snare, which could be tuned and looked "real." And that's where it all started for me. I never lost my enthusiasm and curiosity for music. There were piano players and singers on both sides of my family, so there was encouragement. Even though I would occasionally go in other directions as my school life progressed, my interest never faded. And all these years later, I'm still not over it.

Thom: So, how did your friendship with Billy Joel begin?

Rhys: Well, the scenario was that I had come to the States with my band, and was doing session work for Artie Ripp. He was the one that was the catalyst for my coming together with Billy on the *Cold Spring Harbor* sessions. Don Evans and I were both on these sessions, and it was a neat buzz for me when Larry Knechtel was chosen to play bass because I was familiar with his work, and he was a recording session icon, and this was going to be my first time recording with him. So, we met at the Record Plant in Los Angeles and proceeded to make the *Cold Spring Harbor* album. Artie had brought in Jimmie Haskell to chart all the songs in arrangement form so that he could put the "sweetening" on after the tracks were done, the horns and the strings, et cetera. So, he was kind of like the second musical director, after Billy. At any rate, we proceeded to do the album, and once all the tracks were done, Artie continued on with Jimmie Haskell doing the orchestral sweetening, and Billy and his manager Irwin Mazur went back to New York and waited to hear the finished product.

Thom: This seems like a very elaborate production for such a young artist.

Rhys: Yeah, you know I recently asked someone who was with Billy before *Cold Spring Harbor* the same thing. I was curious because I had never heard what it was like for Billy in anticipation of this record deal. Apparently, he was very excited about coming to L.A., and was looking forward to getting together with this producer to do an album. It seemed that it was a rather big break for someone so young, and he was very enthusiastic about it.

Thom: Regarding the songs themselves, I understand that there was an extensive backlog of material recorded as demos while Billy was under contract. Do you recall how the final running order was determined from that material?

Rhys: Yes, I do. I got a call from Artie Ripp and he said, "I have Billy Joel coming out to do an album, and I have a tape of seven demos that he's already recorded." Some of these were full productions with studio players, and some were just piano/voice. And so, Don Evans and I got together with Artie at his house and he played us the demos—these seven songs that were part of what we were going to do.

Thom: I see.

Rhys: Those songs were from sessions Billy had done in New York, and two of those recordings did survive to the finished album. One was "Why Judy Why" and another was "You Look So Good to Me."

Thom: You know, I've always been curious about that track.

Rhys: Yes, well that was one of the seven demos that I heard. The drummer was Denny Seiwell—a great player. He lives out here on the West Coast and has been out here as long as I have. Anyway, he played great on that track ["You Look So Good to Me"] and I was glad it survived onto the finished LP.

Thom: For sure.

Rhys: Also, I mentioned "Why Judy Why" as another that survived intact from those initial sessions. This song always resonates with me in connection with Billy's classical influences. He started studying at the age of four and thus had that standard instilled in him at an early age. I also grew up listening to piano and a lot of classical music on radio. So, I picked up on that quality in Billy's playing, his songwriting, and particularly in his approach to melody.

Thom: You were talking earlier about Larry Knechtel and Jimmie Haskell. Did Simon & Garfunkel's *Bridge Over Troubled Water* [1970] album have an influence on the sessions for *Cold Spring Harbor*?

Rhys: Well, that album was still riding high on the charts while we were recording with Billy, and I think it did have an influence on our approach. Of course, we did have Larry Knechtel, who was chosen to play bass guitar, and I must admit that Larry seemed a curious choice at the time since he was known mainly as the piano player on "Bridge Over Troubled Water." However, he was also an excellent bass player, and his skill on piano seemed to inform his bass playing. He always seemed able to lock in nicely with Billy's left hand.

Thom: That connection is very interesting.

Rhys: I know. I was totally into that album [*Bridge Over Troubled Water*], and to have Larry Knechtel on bass and Jimmie Haskell orchestrating "Falling of the Rain" and "Tomorrow Is Today" was a real thrill. During the early sessions, Larry, Don Evans, and I came together with Billy to record the basics with arranger Jimmie Haskell, meaning charts, not rehearsals. So, that was an added pressure! But, I'm glad we did that because it gave us a chance to develop various musical gestures in the arrangements that helped bring out the imagery in Billy's lyrics.

Thom: The arrangements are very evocative. Recently, I noticed that wonderful effect on the cymbals at the end of "Falling of the Rain." In keeping with the lyrics of the song, it sounds like the joyful splashing of a puddle. It creates a beautiful soundscape.

Rhys: I love that kind of thing. Always have; always will. And for me, that was a wonderful musical education, and I do thank Artie [Ripp] for giving me the opportunity to discover those kinds of sonic possibilities.

Thom: I understand that Artie was also handling an artist named Kyle who was, at that time, recording an album called *Times That Try a Man's Soul*. Did you work with Kyle as well?

Rhys: Yes, I did, and by the way, I just reconnected with Kyle. It turns out that we were both living in the same town for nearly twenty years, and didn't know it. Go figure. Anyway, through Artie, I worked on tracks for Kyle's album, and some of the other songwriters on his label. So, I've got to give him credit. I spoke with him recently and I asked him flat out, "Artie, do you have that twenty bucks I loaned you?"

Thom [*Laughs*]: Did he?

Rhys [*Laughs*]: No. I also wanted to say, "Since we're talking tabs here, do you have that $200,000 advance we were promised?"

Thom: You know, when I was trying to figure out how to research the details of the *Cold Spring Harbor* sessions, it occurred to me that Artie would be the one who would know. But, then I thought that this was a bad idea because there was so much baggage associated with his initial deal with Billy.

Rhys: Yes, well you know, when I was talking with Artie, I learned that people wanted to interview him about his time with Billy for A&E, or a bio, or something like that. And he said that he declined because, you know, he'd had enough bashing. I totally understand that, and as far as I'm concerned, Thom, that's his and Billy's business.

Thom: Exactly.

Rhys: And I was able to tell Billy's archivist when he asked about all that, I said that I don't feel the need to go into any dirt about Artie. There's no blame game where I am with him. I was given wonderful opportunities through that association.

Thom: As you said earlier, he was the catalyst for your involvement in the *Cold Spring Harbor* sessions.

Rhys: Yes, he was.

Thom: How did the subsequent tour come about?

Rhys: After the *Cold Spring Harbor* tracks were done, while Artie was completing the production and mixing, Billy was putting the band together and needed a drummer. He gave me a call and asked if I wanted to go on the road with him to promote it. At that point, I had yet to play live in the United States, so I eagerly jumped at the opportunity. Billy and I had a very good rapport during the sessions, so it seemed like the logical step.

Thom: I also wanted to ask you about the *Piano Man* sessions. . . .

Rhys: Yes, I did manage to make it onto that album [*laughs*]. I got to play on "Captain Jack."

Thom: I was always impressed with the production team that Michael Stewart put together.

Rhys: Yes, so was I [*laughs*]. Ron Tutt, who had played with Elvis Presley, was Michael's go-to drummer. He also had Wilton Felder from the Crusaders—wonderful bass player. Richard Bennett was on acoustic guitar, and I believe it was Dean Parks on lead guitar on that session. And of course, Michael Omartian was the arranger.

Thom: That's an impressive team.

Rhys: Yes, for sure. During my session, we recorded "Captain Jack," and a version of "The Ballad of Billy the Kid," which wasn't chosen for the final release.

Thom: Did Jimmie Haskell do the orchestrations for the *Piano Man* album?

Rhys: No, Jimmie was only involved on the *Cold Spring Harbor* sessions.[1]

Thom: I see.

Rhys: Did you like what Jimmie added to songs like "Tomorrow Is Today"?

Thom: I think what he did there was brilliant.

Rhys: I do, too.

Thom: Although he became known through the *Bridge Over Troubled Water* sessions for a big kind of orchestration, here he demonstrates a subtle ability with orchestral color. There's a moment on "Tomorrow Is Today" at 1:46 where the low brass enters very quietly under Billy's vocal on the lines "So I listen for an answer, but the feeling seems to stay." It seems to suggest a foreboding light at dawn and portends the next verse where Billy sings, "Still I'm waiting for the morning, but it feels so far away."

Rhys: It is a beautiful moment on that track, I think.

Thom: Another subtle effect is on "Falling of the Rain," the last track on side one of the original LP. Since there is so much activity in the parts, Haskell chooses to shade the entire track with fields of orchestral color. This blends beautifully with the spatial effects evident in your drumming.

Rhys: In the last verse, which begins, "And so the boy becomes a man," it seemed percussively natural to play a full-drums groove behind that lyric and at the same time orchestra-like, creating a finale-force energy of rain and thunder. It was palpable, especially now imagining what Jimmie Haskell was shading with his orchestration.

Thom: Were there string overdubs on other tracks that weren't ultimately used? I thought I could hear faint strings on "She's Got a Way," as if they had been added as an overdub but then mixed out.

Rhys: It's possible that they were added and that Artie or Billy ultimately decided not to include them.

Thom: Were the rhythm tracks recorded live?

Rhys: Yes, all the basic tracks were recorded live—vocals and everything.

Thom: I see.

Rhys: By the way, I don't know if you've noticed, but there is drum bleed on "She's Got a Way." The released mix is piano, bass, and vocal, so the bleed must be coming from my drum part, which ultimately wasn't used. However, I have gotten a sporadic royalty check for playing drums on that song based on CD sales in Japan. In researching those sessions, they evidently got the information that I had played drums on that track, and thought, "Well, he's the drummer so you've got to pay him." And they're right because some of what I was playing leaked through the piano microphones and ended up on the finished recording.

Thom: Wow.

Rhys: But going back to what we were talking about earlier, "She's Got a Way" was one of those pieces that was challenging to me in terms of how one can use percussion to color a track.

Thom: We were chatting a while back about drums as soundscape, and I was wondering if the spread from the piano to the drums could be considered the sound field in which a song really "lives."

Rhys: Yes, I think so. By the way, it was wonderful to re-approach those songs at The Bitter End shows, since I always felt that the arrangements we came up with were quite remarkable.

Thom: A well-known issue with the original release of *Cold Spring Harbor* was the speed of the finished tracks. As I understand it, the multitrack master reel was mixed down to a stereo tape machine that was running slightly slower than normal. Thus, the finished mixes are all slightly sharp when played on a properly calibrated machine. However, I assume that there was no such problem with the multitrack master. Is that true?

Rhys: Well, I wasn't around for the final mixing, so I can't really shed light on any of that. Something definitely did happen with the speed on some of the tracks, but back then it was not uncommon to raise the pitch of the lead vocal on a pop record.

Thom: How was that commonly done?

Rhys: Well, using oscillators, the track would be slowed down before recording the vocal. When the track was then brought back to normal speed, the vocal would have a brighter quality, the kind that was usually associated with the "pop" sound. It's possible that Artie tried to use that technique on the final mix, but as I said, I wasn't around for that part of the process.

Thom: What did you think of Billy's subsequent collaborations with Phil Ramone?

Rhys: I thought that was a perfect marriage of artistic sensibilities. You know, when I played a copy of *The Stranger* [1977], it was the first time I'd really listened to Billy's work in a while. I didn't really bother about *Turnstiles* [1976], partly out of a wounded ego, because I had played a lot of those songs as they were developing. Billy owed Columbia an album, and he had come to that place with Michael Stewart in which he felt that it was time to get back to New York. He'd been in L.A. for a few years, and couldn't really connect with the culture. I could understand that because when I first came to America from New Zealand, I was mixing with people from the New York culture who were in L.A., and I found that I could relate to the New York sensibility much more easily. This may be due to the fact that New York is clearly a city. Where is the city in L.A.? Well, it's downtown—somewhere. It's miles and miles—over there. But Manhattan *is* Manhattan, which is one of the things I personally love about you guys back there. It's one of the things that endeared me to Billy, and vice versa.

Thom: Maybe that's why he worked so well with Phil Ramone. As a New Yorker, Phil understood Billy in a way that Michael Stewart never could.

Rhys: I think so, yes.

Thom: But, to give Stewart his due, Billy seemed a far more confident singer and pianist coming out of *Piano Man* and *Streetlife Serenade* than when he was going into the *Cold Spring Harbor* sessions.

Rhys: Yes, well I think that *Cold Spring Harbor* presented a new set of challenges, and like any musician starting out, he was anticipating that all the ducks were going to line up, and all the planets, and every other jackpot dream of the music business, you know, hit records, et cetera. Did I just say that? [*Laughs*]

Thom: [*Laughs*] Yes.

Rhys: So yeah, as musicians we're all looking to push ahead, and I could tell that Billy was at that point in his career. He was now dealing with the realities of the business. Unfortunately, for a number of reasons, things didn't pan out with Artie. It didn't work, and he found himself in a position of having to start again. And, being a talented and intelligent person, I think he was able to balance any insecurity that he might have had with the knowledge that he had come a long way with the *Cold Spring Harbor* experience. In a way, he'd proved that he would be able to carry on in the business—without getting a day job [*laughs*]. He carried on and got a new deal with Columbia and then went on to make both *Piano Man* [1973] and *Streetlife Serenade* [1974] with Michael Stewart. But to answer your question, I'd say yes, by the time he'd finished those two albums he had a tremendous amount of studio and stage experience and had really become a seasoned professional.

Thom: You can really hear the difference.

Rhys: And, by the time you get to *The Stranger* [1977] and the arrival of Phil Ramone, you can hear a new level of assuredness that seems to be the result of all the work that came before. Plus, there is the tightness of the new band, which is great.

Thom: It's the quintessential Billy Joel sound.

Rhys: Yes, and I compared it with what I had experienced in my time with Billy, and it jumped off of the vinyl in leaps and bounds, man.

Thom: It's an extraordinary journey, to be sure. You know, I keep wanting to go back to *Cold Spring Harbor*.

Rhys: Oh, yeah. You can [*laughs*].

Thom: I'm fascinated by how complete it feels. I mean, for a first album it's a remarkable achievement. The fact that he's writing both the music and the lyrics at such a high level of proficiency—and he was only twenty-two!

Rhys: Yes, I said that to my wife the other day. I think the reason Billy attained the level of success that he did is because he has what I call "the Triad." He possesses the lyrical ability, the musical ability, and the voice to deliver it. And so, the success that he's achieved makes perfect sense. And I can't help but feel proud having been a part of that journey and having learned so much from it.

Thom: The Sigma Sound reunion shows that you guys did at The Bitter End were truly remarkable.

Rhys: Thank you.

Thom: I mean, to hear songs from *Cold Spring Harbor* performed live by the musicians who helped create them was like a dream come true. And the room had such a wonderful vibe. It was really extraordinary.

Rhys: Yes, it was, and I knew that we could do this because the magic is still there. As a tribute to the brilliance of Billy's talent, I've never forgotten those songs, and I felt that I could re-create them and feel just as enthusiastic about them as when I played them on the Sigma Sound radio concert. And that's a unique place for me to be in, you know, having survived it all.

Thom: The quality of the material and those performances are what ultimately led to Billy's contract with Columbia and the *Piano Man* album.

Rhys: Yes, and he was ready. He'd already experienced the United Artists contract with the Hassles and then split off with Jon Small for the Attila project. So, by that point, he was already in the mix in the business. And being the smart person that he is, he was able to retain the best parts of each of those experiences and move forward. When it came to *Piano Man*, he was able to tell the guys at the record label to check it out live, because that's where the proof is with regard to your audience. By then, Billy had been touring for a while and had gained a great deal of confidence in his ability to communicate with an audience. When we were promoting the *Cold Spring Harbor* album, and were opening for major artists, and Billy would perform a solo ballad like "Rosalinda," and be able to put the song over to an audience that had come to see the J. Geils Band.

Thom: That's tough to do.

Rhys: Yes, well he was up to the challenge, and part of his confidence was that he was standing behind his talent.

Thom: You know, I'm glad that his move back to New York involved his exploration of jazz, but I miss the country stuff from his earlier albums.

Rhys: Have you come across a bootleg that's floating around in which Billy goes instantly into a country song, and we all just follow right along? It's an improvised song about a technical difficulty that was occurring at that moment.

Thom: Oh, yes! It was called "Technical Difficulty Blues."

Rhys: Yes, that's it. It was in Memphis. The crew was having trouble with the piano pickup, which I believe was the Helpinstill pickup. This is different from the Barcus Berry system that we eventually used. Anyway, we went through a period with that technology, and the Helpinstill was a pickup that went all the way across the harp of the piano. The concept was that one pickup would cover all eighty-eight keys. Occasionally, with the excessive vibration from performance, sections of the pickup might start to become loose, and would have to be reattached. During one of these issues, Billy went into this country and western thing, and as I said, we all just fell in and started playing along in that style. That was a part of his talent. He could take a scenario of the moment and make a song out of it. You know, we actually did that again in Oyster Bay.

Thom: For a radio show?

Rhys: No, this was when Billy and I got together at his motorcycle shop around the time of The Bitter End shows. I asked him if I could have a photograph of this particular snare drum that I'd been given to play at The Bitter End and World Café shows. Anyway, I asked him if I could get a picture of the snare drum on one of his vintage motorcycles, and he said, "Sure, bring it on in." While we were taking the picture, he started playing the snare drum [*laughs*]. He has the ability to spontaneously create these musical moments. When we first started playing together, we played in Los Angeles at the Troubadour club. During an interlude, Billy started playing a blues and making up a lyric. In the course of that improvisation he mimicked the voices of a whole bunch of people like Johnny Cash, Joe Cocker, and even old vaudevillian actors like George Jessel.

Thom: Wow.

Rhys: These came in handy because at that point, Billy didn't really have forty minutes' worth of material to fill out a set. We were only performing certain songs from the *Cold Spring Harbor* album and a few others that hadn't been recorded. However, he was able to use his ability with voices to create these incredibly entertaining blues pieces. One of these was called "John Wayne Blues." The improvised lyrics referred to various situations such as the technical difficulties in Memphis, and they were entertaining and very impressive. When he had to, he could create these things on the spot.

Thom: At that point, he really seemed to be finding his voice on the piano. During the Hassles and Attila, he was mainly playing the organ.

Rhys: Yeah.

Thom: I recently listened to an obscure song he wrote for the Hassles called "Hotel St. George" and was just blown away by it. It was so impressive for such a young artist, and demonstrated the kind of flexibility you were describing.

Rhys: Huge flexibility. Seeing him again in Oyster Bay and watching him improvise on the snare drum reminded me of that. It was as if the forty-two years that had transpired were totally insignificant.

Thom: Had he heard about the Long, Long Time gigs at The Bitter End and World Café?

Rhys: Yes, when we met at his motorcycle shop that was the first thing he mentioned. I also knew he'd already heard about it because his archivist was at the shows and was sending them to him via the Internet. He complimented our playing and said that what he'd heard was good. He particularly liked "Captain Jack" and acknowledged those cymbal swells [*laughs*].

Thom: There you go [*laughs*].

Rhys: And I told him that, you know, I never got over it [*laughs*]. You'll have to forgive me. I thought it was an example of the "majesticness" he could draw on that was derived from his classical training. Another example of that was "Tomorrow Is Today."

Thom: On the recorded version of "Captain Jack," you do a cymbal roll out of the organ intro.

Rhys: Yes, and by the way, that organ introduction was an overdub that he did at a studio in Burbank that was not that far from Devonshire Sound where the *Piano Man* album was recorded. A distinctive feature of that studio was the fact that they had a cathedral-size organ built in.

And for me, it just doesn't get any better because I grew up loving the cathedral organ and its huge majestic quality.

Thom: It's used in a very subtle manner. It enters quietly so as to give a wonderful sense of space.

Rhys: Yeah, and it wonderfully plays its part on the last chorus out, because the dynamics are at such an incredible level. Part of what was very attractive to Billy live in terms of color was during those early times when we would open for people like the Beach Boys. They loved Billy and quickly told their agency that they wanted him as their opening act. Part of it was his talent, but another aspect was that we'd heard from their sound people how much fun it was to play with the contrast between the large stage show of the Beach Boys versus the small ensemble of a quartet. And yet, they found that they could match that big quality of the Beach Boys' sound with what we were doing.

Thom: It all comes down to orchestration within the ensemble.

Rhys: And dynamics, of course.

Thom: Yes. It's cool that it was the 1971–1972 era Beach Boys, which was a very hip period for them. They seemed to be totally in sync with the counterculture.

Rhys: Yeah, and being a New Zealander, I was beside myself because, you know, I was hanging out with Dennis Wilson.

Thom: That's amazing.

Rhys: A few years down the line, Billy was the catalyst for me drumming with the Beach Boys at the Spectrum in Philly. Dennis was coming back to do an encore, and as he's coming back around onstage, he hands me the drumsticks and says, "Get up there and play. I'm going out front."

Thom: Beautiful.

Rhys: Yeah. Thanks for indulging me, Thom [laughs].

Thom: My pleasure. It's great.

Rhys: So, enough of me. I love where you're coming from in terms of getting a little feedback on the journey from Artie Ripp to Phil Ramone. I'm glad to be able to talk about it, as you can tell.

Thom: I appreciate it. It's a remarkable body of work that was produced in those few years.

Rhys: Yeah, well Artie knew what he was getting. He could hear the potential on those original seven demos.

Thom: I've been trying to understand how that whole system worked. What I mean is how did Clive Davis know Artie, and how did Larry Knechtel and Jimmie Haskell get to play on the *Cold Spring Harbor* sessions? I think we need to know more about how that whole network evolved.

Rhys: Yeah, it's a small village when it comes to that, and Artie had come out to the small village known as Los Angeles, and Hollywood, and Beverly Hills. He brought that thing that it takes to establish your own new world, and that is, you know, money. So, Artie was carrying on and getting into being the head of everything—of the family, so to speak. So, consequently, I got swept up in it like Billy did, and it just didn't work.

Thom: What was Artie doing before Family Productions?

Rhys: I only knew that he had previously been with Kama Sutra of Buddah/Kama Sutra. And part of their success at the time was the bubblegum stuff like Lemon Pipers, and 1910 Fruitgum Company. So, when he came out to the West Coast, Artie was just trying to get in there as well. He wanted to be a Lou Adler, you know what I mean?

Thom: Sure.

Rhys: Lou Adler produced the Mamas and the Papas, and had just done *Tapestry* for Carole King. Artie wanted to be in that mix, and he had the money source to be able to do that. When we first started out, he knew what he'd heard in Billy, plus, he had an association with Woodstock at that time, which was also an association with Michael Lang. Now, Michael Lang, I believe, was where those first seven demos came from.

Thom: I see.

Rhys: Michael Lang was one of those who helped organize the Woodstock concert. So, when we joined up with Artie he was riding high on that. He would be wearing the Woodstock logo on his T-shirt.

Thom: Very hip.

Rhys: Yeah, it was. And, he'd be driving this Excalibur that he'd bought. That's when he first came to see my band, and decided he liked what he'd heard and signed us. For us, Artie's association with Woodstock and Michael Lang enhanced the dream, you know. Plus, he had Kama Sutra. So, what I'm saying is, when we first started talking about Billy's reaction to his forthcoming deal, as it were, apparently he had the same enthusiasm. It seemed to everyone concerned like a real good shot with a guy who's in L.A. and has all the ways and means.

Thom: The kind of a guy who could plug you in to the system.

Rhys: Yeah, he could be the path, and Billy was apparently genuinely excited about that. After what he'd been through with the Hassles and Attila, it must have seemed like a great opportunity. Billy didn't show any discouragement, which was good. Instead, he showed that he wanted to pursue this thing and was confident in the power of his talent. He was already there and let's face it—his DNA contains it.

Thom: Yes, there was always an acknowledgment of his dad's abilities as a pianist, but I used to wonder where the voice came from. I heard later that his mom had been a singer.

Rhys: Yeah, so there you go. Billy set a fine example of someone who recognized what he'd inherited, and made something of it. His daughter Alexa is doing the same thing.

Thom: I've often thought about how musical training and cultural circumstance can create pressure to follow a certain sound. Now and again, artists seem to emerge out of nowhere with a fully formed and original approach. Even though Billy had traditional training, he seems to fall into the latter group in that he was able to carve a very unique path.

Rhys: Yes, he has the ability to go into those different musical bags and come up with something that is listenable, approachable, and has incredible sophistication.

Thom: If it's okay, I wanted to run something by you with regard to the *Streetlife Serenade* album.

Rhys: Sure.

Thom: One of my favorite songs on that album was "Last of the Big Time Spenders."

Rhys: Yeah, good song.

Thom: So, I'm listening to the lead vocal and suddenly thought I could hear the influence of Rita Coolidge on the way Billy was phrasing. I remember that as being a trick for male singers to emulate female vocalists. For some reason, the listener has a hard time spotting an influence that goes across genders. I know Rita had been a prominent musical artist in L.A. when Billy was out there, so it seemed to make sense.

Rhys: It's very possible, because he can do that very easily. I've always said that he does Joe Cocker better than Joe himself. It's a good element that he's kept—the freedom to play around with his voice and to bring the audience along with him. He gives you, as the listener, the feeling that he wants you to be a part of it.

Thom: He really seems to enjoy that dynamic.

Rhys: Yes, he has a wonderful communication with the audience that he's able to build on during the performance. It's a gift.

Thom: Well, thank you for taking the time to speak with me, Rhys.

Rhys: My pleasure.

APPENDIX C

Interview with Don Evans
October 2, 2014

Thom: Hi Don, how are you?

Don: I'm good. Can you hear me okay?

Thom: I can hear you perfectly.

Don: Too much echo?

Thom: No, it sounds great.

Don: So, who else have you talked to? You've talked to Rhys?

Thom: I talked to Rhys earlier this summer.

Don: Rhys's memory is much better than mine [*laughs*]. I'm not kidding, though. He's much more clear. I've never had an incredible memory anyway, and a lot of that stuff, for many reasons, is fading.

Thom: I'm fascinated by this period in Joel's career. First of all, *Cold Spring Harbor* sounded to me like a proto-indie album—the type of artistry one would expect to hear in the early '90s.

Don: Have you heard the actual LP version from '71 as opposed to the remixed version from the early '80s?

Thom: Yes, I had a copy of the original release.

Don: Well, they're very different. When Artie [Ripp] remixed it, he recorded over a lot of the tracks. Rhys's drums aren't even on a lot of the tracks.

Thom: The remix sounded very '80s on one level, and on another, like a demo album.

Don: He really wrecked it.

Thom: One of the things I love about the original album was the beautiful blend of sensibilities. Rhys and I talked about the influence of *Bridge Over Troubled Water* on the production style.

Don: Joe Osborn and Larry Knechtel were on both albums.

Thom: And Jimmie Haskell.

Don: Right.

Thom: Rhys pointed out that *Bridge Over Troubled Water* was still very much in circulation during the sessions for *Cold Spring Harbor*. I've often wondered if it influenced the spirit of creativity that seems evident on those sessions.

Don: I think so. I particularly remember the spontaneity. A song that stands out in that regard is "You Can Make Me Free." Billy sang it, and we played it. I was standing near him as he played his piano. I used my old Super Reverb, which I still have. The studio guys had a setup where the guitar amp was pointed into a bass trap and then they basically built a fort around it. The lid on Billy's piano was opened with just enough room to get the microphones in, and then it was completely covered. It was a pretty dated recording method. Some of the things they were doing back then were very misguided. The isolation they achieved was almost enough, but if you listen to the remixed version, you can hear echoes of my guitar lines before they're actually there. Despite their efforts there was some leakage. So, Billy sang, and we played—and that was it.

Thom: Wow.

Don: Recently, I was talking with this kid from the *Billy Joel Completely Retold* Facebook page. He said that he thought "You Can Make Me Free" was one of the best guitar solos ever, but I was just trying to make a good impression! [*Laughs*] It was early in the project and I was just trying to make it clear that I could play, you know, and just trying to do it right. Billy was totally inspirational. I think the first song we ever played to warm up might have been the Joe Cocker version of "She Came In Through the Bathroom Window," which was followed by a series of different songs that we all knew. I think we might have finished up with "Feelin' Alright."

Thom: He played "Feelin' Alright" on Chip Monck's *Speakeasy* TV show in 1974 and he sounded just like Joe Cocker!

Don: Well, he's done all that stuff. He has a great facility with voices. He can imitate anybody.

Thom: I remember reading that at the time Billy and John Belushi were the best Joe Cocker imitators around.

Don: Billy was better than any of them. He could do James Taylor, Leon Russell, Elton John, et cetera. Every once in a while I hear a bootleg where he's really doing this stuff. I think that maybe I was more impressed at the time than I would be now, but no, he was great. He could capture the essence of McCartney and a lot of other people as well.

Thom: The McCartney comparison has been used quite a bit—aptly so, because he was clearly an influence—but in terms of his writing, I find that McCartney is a bit messier than Billy, if you know what I mean. Billy's pieces are so together. When I look closely at the counterpoint in his songs, I'm amazed at how tight it is.

Don: He had a head for it on top of a lot of classical training. It's funny, but at the time he was denying it, or minimizing it, at least. Beyond that, he also had an incredible ability to recall gestures, if you will, from any musical style. I mean, I don't know if anyone actually taught him about jazz ballads but he could remember what he'd heard and bring those gestures into a song like "New York State of Mind." Remarkable.

Thom: When I spoke with guitarist/composer Ira Newborn, he described getting together with Billy when they were teenagers to read through *The Real Book* of standards. He also said that Billy would often play him original songs that were very impressive.

Don: That makes sense. He definitely wanted Frank Sinatra to record "New York State of Mind." That was one of his goals.

Thom: What else do you remember about the *Cold Spring Harbor* sessions?

Don: I remember doing the acoustic guitar on "Everybody Loves You Now." That was actually rather stressful because when I cut it with the full band, they couldn't get enough separation, so I had to redo the part as an overdub.

Thom: That particular track seemed to make quite an impact at the time.

Don: It was a single.

Thom: It seems like there's a James Taylor vibe on the song "Turn Around."

Don: Very much so. Actually, there were a few times he played it where he sounded exactly like Taylor. People would criticize him for that kind of thing, but I thought it was cool that he could put on a "James Taylor suit" and do a song in that style.

Thom: The Harry Chapin sound also seems to be a factor.

Don: Actually, we did some gigs with Harry. That was interesting. He was one of the people that critics wanted to lump Billy in with, especially after the *Piano Man* album. Even though his first big hit was a story song, Billy's attitude was, "Hey, I'm not a storyteller." Actually, he seemed to be more of a character artist. He would paint pictures kind of like Gordon Lightfoot.

Thom: And Randy Newman?

Don: Actually, he's more like Mark Knopfler, I think. Knopfler tends to paint pictures of people and events—kind of like mini-movies. To me, that's closer to the way Billy worked.

Thom: I wanted to ask you about the Long, Long Time reunion shows at The Bitter End last year. I was there and the vibe in the room was amazing.

Don: Thanks. It was really interesting playing that show, because on a personal level, there was good stuff and bad stuff about being in that band. The memories were all pretty good until we actually got onstage, and feelings of frustration with certain things began to surface. In Billy's band, you were very much a sideman. Someone recently told me that he thought we helped make Billy, but that's not true. We were just the people that were there. If it hadn't been me, it would have been somebody else. That's how all of life is, really. The door opens and you happen to be standing there, you walk through, and there you are. That's very much how it was with Billy. It wasn't a process of getting there. It was just that suddenly, the opportunity to play with Billy was there.

Thom: There seemed to be a comfort level in that band that was evident at The Bitter End shows. Recently, someone posted a TV appearance from a university in the Midwest, and you could see it there as well.

Don: It could have been University of Southern Illinois. You know, when we were out on the road we were very much a band. Regarding the business side of it, there's a certain kind of thing, a solvency that has to be there. Otherwise, it fails. But while you're out there, you can't really be thinking about that. You just have to focus on the people in the band. The first tours I was on with Billy, we were three abreast in two station wagons with all of our gear in the back. It was as unglamorous as it could possibly be. You become these musical commandos, and you think of yourself that way. "We're taking this town; we're taking that town." In the process, you experience each other in all kinds of ways. You become a family.

Thom: Do you think the challenges of that kind of lifestyle make the music better?

Don: That's a romantic view. Maybe.

Thom: Let me ask you about the conception of the music on *Cold Spring Harbor*. There are so many interesting influences flowing through the music, and this was also very evident at the Long, Long Time shows. We talked earlier about *Bridge Over Troubled Water* looming in the background, so the influence of Paul Simon is likely. At the same time, parts of "Tomorrow Is Today" seem to recall Jimmy Webb.

Don: Well, we've been talking about touring so let me point out that my experience on the road with Billy was post–*Piano Man*. I played on the *Cold Spring Harbor* album, and then went on to work on other projects. I was still working with the guys who had been in the Trade Winds. They were a New York session group and we had cut what were known at the time as "bubblegum" records back in New York.

Thom: "New York's a Lonely Town."

Don: Right. I was not on that record. I got together with them a bit later. The guitar player in that band, Jimmy Calvert, was starting to produce, and he put the word out that he wanted somebody to come in and work with them in his place while he was on the other side of the glass. A friend of his was Barry Singer, the manager of Rondo's Music in Union, New Jersey. When Barry was asked for a referral, the first name out of his mouth was mine. So, Jimmy told him to send me in, and I cut a bunch of tracks with them, including stuff for the Ohio Express. I was also on "Montego Bay" by Bobby Bloom.

Thom: You were on "Montego Bay"?

Don: Yeah, and by the way, there are no actual steel drums on that record. We got that sound by having one player hitting vibes, and another hitting on garbage can lids.

Thom: Wow.

Don: So, there were a few. Once in a while, I hear myself on a song that's playing in a 7/11, or Wawa's. The late-night music in Wawa's seems especially tuned in to this kind of material [*laughs*]. Anyway, that band went to L.A. to work with Artie Ripp, and in hindsight, I think he thought that we were going to be his "Wrecking Crew." Everybody was trying to do that, because Phil [Spector] had his guys, and I guess Artie wanted to emulate Phil.

Thom: So, Artie had been at Buddah/Kama Sutra before coming to L.A.?

Don: Yes.

Thom: Recently, I learned that Artie was working with Lovin' Spoonful at the time they recorded "Do You Believe in Magic."

Don: Artie Ripp had a thing for "Do You Believe in Magic." He always believed that it should have been a bigger hit, and he persuaded a lot of his artists to cover it. He just felt that it never became the classic that it should have been.

Thom: That's interesting.

Don: As a producer, Artie made expensive records. Most of the records back then were cut pretty quick, if not all the way live they were mostly live. You went into the studio for three hours and you came out with a single or two. The '70s hadn't quite started, but Artie was very much going in that direction, you know, camping out in the studio forever. The people with the money weren't ready to let him do that. Anyway, I had done a session with him back in New York, and he had already hired the band. They were all there, and he brought out this tape by an artist he had named Kyle, and . . .

Thom: Kyle! His album was called *Times That Try a Man's Soul* [1971].

Don: That's him. He had a song called "Black Gets Blacker" that I was overdubbing on. We went straight through the song producing a solid take, but Artie wanted to re-do the guitar solo. So, we worked on it for three more hours, the same twelve bars over and over again. Finally, I played what I thought was clearly my best work ever. Artie said, "Don, that was incredible, but I feel like the next one is going to be the phenomenal one." At this point, I'm almost in tears. I'm ready to throw my guitar through the control room window. So, I just put it down, walked out of the door, walked downstairs, walked down the block for a while, and then came back. By then, I had calmed down and was able to finish it. After that session he asked us to come out to Los Angeles as his studio band, and Billy was one of his artists. So, I actually met Billy a few days before we went into the studio to record *Cold Spring Harbor*. I heard some of the material that he had already cut back in New York, like "You Look So Good to Me," and "Why Judy Why."

Thom: Did Sal De Troia play guitar on "Why Judy Why"?

Don: Yes. Beautiful work.

Thom: I was recently trying to write about "You Look So Good to Me" and had a lot of trouble pinning down the influence. The Rascals influence was detectable, but also a touch of Lovin' Spoonful.

Don: Very Long Island, I'd say.

Thom: I see.

Don: So, that's how the Billy Joel thing happened. Artie introduced us, and we started working together, and I was trying to be the guy that I was expected to be. After the album, he went out on tour for seven months, or more, and Artie paid for that. He put them up in all these incredible hotels like the Plaza in New York City—all these really cool places. Then, it's my understanding that they got home and it was like a scene out of an old music business movie. The band members expected to be paid, but instead they were presented with all the bills for the expenses they had incurred on the road. Billy stopped going on the road at that point. For numerous reasons, Billy basically said to Artie, "Screw this, I'm not doing this anymore." He went underground and did that famous gig at the Executive Lounge in Los Angeles. I had no contact with him during this time. I had been going off to work with the guys from the Trade Winds. By the time Billy was done with his Executive Lounge thing, I was working at a music repair shop called Valley Sound, repairing guitars and pianos. One day, Billy walked in with his Wurlitzer piano under his arm, saw me, and said, "You!" We hadn't been in touch, but he asked me to come play with his band, and I said yes.

Thom: So, the *Cold Spring Harbor* band was one band, and the one that toured after the *Piano Man* album was another?

Don: Yes, and at this point, they didn't have a bass player, either. The first bass player we had was actually a friend of mine. I had kind of put together a small band trying to get something going and I had Patrick MacDonald as my bass player (not the famous Patrick MacDonald). Patrick was working with people that I had been working with in that two-year period, and he asked if he could fill the bass slot in Billy's band. So, we told him to come over and play, and he got the gig. Doug Stegmeyer ultimately replaced him. Rhys played the drums throughout those two phases of Billy's band. The first time I played with Larry Russell was when we did the Long, Long Time reunion shows. As I said, I was not involved in the first phase of Billy's touring band. That was Al Hertzberg, who is a really good guitar player. His style is sort of along the lines of Jeff Beck.

Thom: Didn't Al Hertzberg play on *Streetlife Serenade*?

Don: He played the guitar solo on the title track, which is a great solo. As far as I know, that's the only track he's on. I played on "The Entertainer," "Weekend Song," and maybe one other. I can't recall.

Thom: For a long time, *Streetlife Serenade* was my favorite Billy Joel album. I just loved the sound of that record. It seemed so colorful. Where did that stuff come from?

Don: As far as I know, every song Billy had written after *Cold Spring Harbor* was on that record. At that point, he wasn't particularly prolific. I'm not sure why. He seemed to get more prolific later on, although, I think we've probably heard everything he's ever written. He doesn't really churn them out.

Thom: He does have a habit of writing entire albums. He sits down and writes ten or more songs that become the album. Quite remarkable, I think.

Don: Well, from what I remember about Billy, the music was easy and the lyric was hard. He could do melodies forever. It's interesting, though. With regard to his lyrics, I could spot a lot of real life in there, even after our time together. For instance, I could identify the main character of "Big Shot" right down to all the little details. And I'm sure that all the people described in "Piano Man" were based on people who were really there.

Thom: With regard to "Piano Man," I had the 45 rpm single when it first came out. That was the edited version. A few years later, I heard the full version of the song on the *Piano Man* album. It seemed epic in comparison with the single edit—his "Desolation Row."

Don: You know what, we just got back to something. You were talking earlier about influences on the music. After *Piano Man,* there was a tendency to lump him in there with people like Jim Croce or Harry Chapin. In other words, he was being tagged as a storytelling songwriter, and he kind of resisted that. He didn't want to be thought of in that way. He also didn't want to be the next Elton John. I mean, their names were right next to each other in the record rack. He could do a good Elton John impression, but was always quick to point out the differences.

Thom: It's been asserted that the overall concept for the *Piano Man* album was derived from Elton's *Tumbleweed Connection.*

Don: That album could have inspired a few of the tracks because we had definitely heard it—Elton's first album too, the one with the big orchestrations. And speaking of orchestration, the band Yes was a huge influence on Billy. Everything he heard that was orchestral, he kind of wanted to do. At the same time, we would listen to instrumental records from back when we were kids, things like "The Lonely Surfer" by Jack Nitzsche. He was not limited in any way musically. If he wanted to do it, he would just do it.

Thom: A track like "The Mexican Connection" from *Streetlife Serenade* has elements of jazz, country and western, and even Aaron Copland via Elmer Bernstein. Plus, the opening riff comes from "Catch a Falling Star" by Perry Como! Wonderful track.

Don: Oh, yeah, he used that as his opening-the-show music, and we sometimes took over live in the middle.

Thom: I've been thinking a lot about the Michael Stewart sessions. On *Cold Spring Harbor,* he sounds young. I mean, everybody's young on that album, right? I wouldn't say that he sounds wild, but it seems like he still has to settle down a bit. Then, when he comes out of the sessions for *Piano Man* and *Streetlife Serenade,* he sounds like a seasoned studio pro. I mean, his vocal tracks are just perfect. In retrospect, I began to wonder if Michael Stewart had been putting him through the numbers throughout the sessions for those two albums, in a sense, getting him to hone his chops a bit more.

Don: Interesting. Speaking to that, there are versions of "The Entertainer" that were made before we officially recorded it. And on those versions, Billy doesn't play at all until the end. Then, Michael came in and completely changed it. He made it more of a piano record . . . the rhythm guitar part did survive, though.

Thom: That's you playing the acoustic rhythm guitar part?

Don: Yeah. I had been doing "Everybody Loves You Now" on the road all that time, which has a similar kind of drive to it. I always had that Richie Havens kind of thing, anyway, that whole kind of—you probably can't hear this. [*Don begins to demonstrate the rhythm guitar part from "The Entertainer"*]

Thom: I can hear it. It sounds great!

Don: [*Continuing to play*] On one of those earlier versions I mentioned, I was playing this insane stuff—but unlike now, I was really keeping time [*laughs*]. I mean, I listen to it now and it still sounds like a hard part to play.

Thom: It's a tough part and it goes straight though the song!

Don: So, we get all the way through "The Entertainer," and it's not until the last two verses that Billy is actually playing piano.

Thom: That dramatic entrance toward the end of the song?

Don: Yes, but as far as his vocals go, that's just the way Billy sang it. I wasn't there for the *Piano Man* album, but the level of session players that he got probably gave Michael a level of control that he might not have had otherwise. Who was the arranger? I forget his name.

Thom: Michael Omartian.

Don: That's him.

Thom: Did he do the orchestration on "The Ballad of Billy the Kid"?

Don: I think so, yes.[1]

Thom: I know he often collaborated with Michael Stewart, and worked on the *Piano Man* album, but he wasn't listed on the liner notes for *Streetlife Serenade*.

Don: Really? That's strange, because I think he wrote the charts. They wrote charts for all the songs. They did a lot of preproduction, and then Billy would come in, and we played the stuff down like it was an "old school" recording session. Everyone had their little place where they sat. Chuck Rainey was the bass player on both of the sessions I was on, and Ron Tutt was the drummer.

Thom: What was it like working with Tutt?

Don: He's a great drummer, and actually he shares certain style characteristics with Liberty DeVitto but I preferred working with Rhys . . . we lock up better . . . his time feels better to me.

Thom: And Rhys is atmospheric. I love the way he approaches the kit as a soundscape.

Don: Yes.

Thom: There's not a lot written about Michael Stewart. He was in the band, We Five, who had the hit "You Were on My Mind" in 1965.

Don: I know he was John Stewart's brother.

Thom: Really? John Stewart wrote "Daydream Believer" for the Monkees.

Don: Yes, and I think he was also in the Kingston Trio.

Thom: Not bad, eh? [*Laughs*]

Don: Now I want to go and check this stuff out [*laughs*]. By the way, we did a series of sessions with Michael that constituted an attempt to do a live thing. Those sessions took place at the Great American Music Hall in San Francisco. It was a really awful place to try and record, because it's all granite and terrazzo with this big tile ceiling. So, we recorded a bunch of live stuff there, including "New York State of Mind," and "James." As you know, both of those, re-recorded, ended up on *Turnstiles,* and there were other songs that ended up on subsequent releases. So, I played on the original recording of "New York State of Mind," and some of what I emphasized in my guitar part became what Billy emphasized in his piano part on the released version. That was probably an instinctive response on his part, but it was still a bit frustrating, interesting to hear the finished versions of those songs after we'd worked on developing them.

Thom: It seems like such a chaotic period between *Streetlife Serenade* and *Turnstiles.*

Don: Well, he had moved back east, and was basically intending to move away from Michael. He was moving toward the collaboration with Phil [Ramone], which is exactly what he needed. If you listen to *The Stranger,* that's the first time Billy was actually the real Billy, as far as I was concerned.

Thom: As much as I like that album, I've always been troubled by the way the piano was recorded. I can appreciate why it works in the context of the whole record, but it seems so tinny as compared with the piano sound on the Stewart productions.

Don: Yeah, that's a function of the mix. I think he was trying to drop the piano back a little bit.

Thom: It sounded almost AM to my ears. In other words, it's what piano sounded like on AM radio, or transistor radio. However, that kind of works for the overall sound picture they created for *The Stranger*.

Don: Yeah, you're right, but remember that this was the 1970s, so there were limitations. I should also mention that in addition to being a guitarist, I'm also a recording engineer, so, I think I understand how the piano on *The Stranger* got to sound like that. It's an attitude, as much as anything: trying to bring it up in the mix; trying to make it lock in. I suppose that "AM" would be a good way to describe the resulting sound.

Thom: Yes, I think so. By the way, these are just observations about why the production technique might resonate with an audience that grew up on AM radio. On a personal level, I am very much on the side of playing with the materials in order to shape, or find, the sound.

Don: I think it's like recording an acoustic guitar, which is very tough to record because it sounds different from wherever you listen to it. You can put microphones all over the place to try to get a good sound. Then, when you go to mix it, you roll most of the bottom, because it's in the way of everything else. You try to get it to sit with the bass and to sit with the kick drum, and I think that's what Phil was doing with the piano on *The Stranger* album. He was mixing for the whole record with the vocal up front. As a result, he may have had to trash the piano sound a bit to get the vocal up front.

Thom: That's interesting in light of the fact that Billy doesn't like to record vocals away from the keyboard.

Don: Yes, he prefers to sing while he's playing. That's another thing, too. If you're recording both simultaneously, inevitably, one will suffer.

Thom: We're still in the process of trying to evolve a way of talking about the connections between recording technique and compositional process. It seems to me that the engineer has to approach the multi-track recording in a manner similar to the way an orchestrator approaches a musical score.

Don: You know, a long time ago, a really good engineer that I worked with told me that a good mix has more to do with the arrangement than it does with the mix itself. Good sounds on a recording have more to do with the arrangement than with your skills as a recording engineer. If you think about the records that sound the best, it's because you're allowed to hear everything. The more I would engineer, the more impatient I would become with bad arrangements.

Thom: In other words, you shouldn't have to fix it at the mixing console. It should be part of the overall process.

Don: Yes, you should be able to put the faders up and hear something that sounds right. Then, it just becomes a matter of tweaking and massaging the sound. So, absolutely with regard to what you're saying, it's all about arranging. My favorite bands are the ones in which their songs come off like an orchestral piece as opposed to a rock band going through the numbers. Billy's stuff has that kind of cohesion, I think.

Thom: Going back to your comment about acoustic guitars, and connecting again with the *Bridge Over Troubled Water* album, the acoustic guitars on "The Boxer" are very well recorded. I think it was Paul Simon and Fred Carter Jr. playing those parts around one microphone. Good sound.

Don: Yeah, but did you know that they were using little guitars on that session?

Thom: I didn't know that.

Don: Yes. Actually, when Paul Simon had his guitar made, Guild made two. The other one was given to a guy named Peter Anders, who was involved with the whole group of people that I was involved with, like Vini Poncia. By the way, Anders and Poncia were a songwriting team. So, I got to play the other Paul Simon guitar, and it was like a single-ought Martin, a little tiny thing. Those guitars tend to sound better on a recording, because you can get the microphones very close to them and get a really big, full sound.

Thom: Regarding the sound of the piano, I began to wonder if the realism of the Michael Stewart production style works against Billy's songwriting aesthetic.

Don: It's unromantic, I think.

Thom: Stewart's approach?

Don: Yes.

Thom: It's very dry, and professional, and precise, but at odds with the Edward Hopper–like vision that seems evident on the cover of *Streetlife Serenade*. Later, he realizes that vision on *The Stranger* with Phil Ramone.

Don: I agree. I think that's what it is with *The Stranger,* and pretty much everything since. There's been a certain romantic vision. The piano sound may be a factor, but the whole sound picture is amazing. That's what hadn't really happened with Michael Stewart, and it didn't happen on *Turnstiles*, either.

Thom: More and more, *Turnstiles* seems transitional. There's a bland quality about the sound of that album that bothers me. I like "James," but that particular track is so basic in its layout, it wouldn't need to be fussed over. However, on something like "Prelude/Angry Young Man," the mix sounds rather flat.

Don: Yes, and I think part of that is the recording, and part of it is the production. I think they needed someone on the sessions other than Billy or the engineer. Someone who could ask questions like, "Why aren't those piano hammers hitting me in the face?" They didn't have that, and as a result, the album sounds like a demo—a very, very good demo, I think.

Thom: This is interesting, because I was originally leaning toward calling *Cold Spring Harbor* a demo album, but it really isn't.

Don: It's different.

Thom: There seems to be a clear production idea. It starts off with the simplicity of "She's Got a Way," followed by the wonderful drive of "Everybody Loves You Now." Then, into the weather world of "Falling of the Rain," that leads towards the full orchestration of "Tomorrow Is Today." In comparison, the *Turnstiles* album seems somehow incomplete.

Don: I'm afraid it might sound like I'm overly critical, having been involved in the *Cold Spring Harbor* album, but I think you're right. I think *Turnstiles* was a transitional album, and it clearly demonstrates why it was a good idea for him to get together with Phil [Ramone].

Thom: The premise of this book is that there is a discernible arc between *Cold Spring Harbor* [1971] and *The Stranger* [1977]. I'm hearing *The Stranger* as an endpoint rather than a point of departure. I don't envy him having to start over following that record. *52nd Street* [1978] was a good follow-up, but after that it seems to become more of a challenge. How do you sustain? Where do you go?

Don: It's like the Beatles after *Sgt. Pepper*. I think that whatever it was that sparked the Beatles in their later works, that's what Billy needed to have in the studio. He needed that kind of atmosphere and openness, and I think that Phil provided that, and helped him find what he was looking for. By the way, Billy takes a bad rap for using a lot of different styles, but all the styles that he adopted were all him. He wasn't derivative; he was multifaceted.

Thom: He was eclectic.

Don: Yes, and that was a bad thing to be at the time. You were much better off if you were like a James Taylor or a Jim Croce, doing one particular style.

Thom: In connection with the role of the producer, I've written about how the Beatles, with George Martin to encourage them, embraced the recording studio as a compositional tool. This doesn't seem to be as much the case with Billy. I've heard a few demos, but not many. He's always been very involved in the planning of the album concept, but unlike the Beatles, he hasn't seemed as interested in the recording process itself.

Don: I think he got more involved as time went on, but you're right. In those days, much of the time he was being produced. Regarding Artie [Ripp], the problem in that situation was that, with all due respect to Artie, he didn't know when the project was done. In those first *Cold Spring Harbor* sessions, the truth of it was that Artie brought together a band that had very good chemistry, and put them together with a really good artist. Then, we took the bit in our teeth and ran with it. That's how that stuff was cut. It was the band and Billy. We hadn't met before, and had hardly played together, if at all. Actually, our first time playing together was in the studio.

Thom: Rhys mentioned that Artie seemed to be envisioning himself as another Lou Adler.

Don: Or, Phil Spector.

Thom: Yes!

Don: As I said earlier, he wanted us to be his "Wrecking Crew," but it didn't happen. I mean, we were not Joe Osborn, or Hal Blaine, et cetera. We were not those people.

Thom: They were the kind of players that would live in the studio and be on all the sessions.

Don: Yes, that's what he thought he had found.

Thom: I see.

Don: So, Billy was one of his artists, but there were others as well.

Thom: Yes, you mentioned Kyle earlier.

Don: Rhys actually got back together with Kyle recently.

Thom: He mentioned that when I spoke with him. He said they discovered that they lived within a few miles of one another.

Don: Yeah, I'm on the fence about that sort of thing. There are some things you want to revisit, and there are certain things you don't.

Thom: In other words, maybe it's just meant to be this way, so leave it alone.

Don: People ask me if I'm in contact with Billy. Not really, but I can remember being in Billy's dressing room when someone from the old days was trying to get in, and Billy ducked out the other side because he didn't want to deal with it. It's a compartmentalizing kind of thing, and I understand it.

Thom: Makes sense.

Don: I've been at shows, and I do get shout-outs from the stage. He played Philly and I went to the Valentine's Day show. My wife got tickets for it, and took *me* to see Billy Joel [*laughs*]. And that's another thing—I'm reluctant to ask him to get me tickets for a show, because I know how he felt about it. Some people think of it as cheap, but I don't. You don't come back and try to take advantage of someone you used to work with.

Thom: He's just a guy. My attitude is that he did a good job. Well done.

Don: If I could do anything, I would want to sit in a room, have a cup of coffee with him, whatever, and just say, "Dude, you did great." He's an amazing character, and he's someone that I'm very glad to have worked with.

Thom: Thank you very much for taking the time to talk with me, Don.

Don: My pleasure.

NOTES

PREFACE

1. Chuck Klosterman, *Sex, Drugs, and Cocoa Puffs: A Low Culture Manifesto*, 44.

2. Shio, "History of Live Performances by Billy Joel," *Glass Houses:* Billy Joel Web Page, https://web.archive.org/web/20130116171147/http://www.shio.org/BJ/concerts/#1977.

3. In case you were wondering, I grew up on 52nd Street in Bayonne.

4. "Remembering You" by Roger Kellaway and Carroll O'Connor is best known as the closing theme to the television series *All in the Family*.

5. Mannes College of Music, 157 East 74th St., New York.

6. At the 2008 Art of Record Production conference held at University of Massachusetts, Lowell, I spoke briefly with producer Phil Ramone, who validated the significance of this perceived connection. He pointed out that the Rhodes piano I was hearing on both tracks was the same—his own!

I. A PORTRAIT OF THE ARTIST

1. Fred Schruers, *Billy Joel: The Definitive Biography*, 16–20.

2. Billy Joel, *Inside the Actors Studio*, episode 6.1, directed by Jeff Wurtz, VHS.

3. Hank Bordowitz, *Billy Joel: The Life and Times of an Angry Young Man*, 6.

4. Billy Joel, "In Conversation with Judy Carmichael," *Judy Carmichael's Jazz Inspired*, 2000, http://www.jazzinspired.com/#/billy-joel/.

5. Schruers, *Billy Joel*, 23–25.

6. Bordowitz, *Billy Joel*, 7–8.

7. Schruers, *Billy Joel*, 17.

8. Ibid., 41.

9. Ira Newborn (musician and composer), discussion with the author, November 20, 2013.

10. Schruers, *Billy Joel*, 35.

11. Walter Everett, "Beatles, the." *Grove Music Online*, n.d., http://ezproxy. library.nyu.edu:2611/subscriber/article/grove/music/A2223785.

12. Bordowitz, *Billy Joel*, 17.

13. Denis O'Dell, *At the Apple's Core: The Beatles from the Inside*, 102.

14. Schruers, *Billy Joel*, 35.

15. Bordowitz, *Billy Joel*, 19.

16. "Billboard, Aug 15, 1964, p. 5," Google Books, https://books.google. com/books?id=QUUEAAAAMBAJ&pg=PA5&dq=artie+ripp&hl=en&sa=X& ved=0CDQQ6AEwBjhQahUKEwjayPLo4uXIAhVF7R4KHUq8B5c#v= onepage&q=artie%20ripp&f=false.

17. Bordowitz, *Billy Joel*, 23–30.

18. Schruers, *Billy Joel*, 59–61.

19. Ibid,. 71.

20. Bordowitz, *Billy Joel*, 41–42.

21. Ibid., 48.

22. Bob Hyde, "The Kama Sutra/Buddah Records Story," *Both Sides Now Stereo Newsletter,* n.d., http://www.bsnpubs.com/buddah/buddahstory.html.

23. Rhys Clark (musician), discussion with the author, June 9, 2014.

24. Ibid.

25. Andy Childs, "Billy Joel: Piano Man," *ZigZag*, July 1975, Rock's Backpages, EBSCOhost.

26. Clark, discussion with the author, June 9, 2014.

27. Don Evans (musician), discussion with the author, October 2, 2014.

28. Ibid.

29. Schruers, *Billy Joel*, 78.

30. Bordowitz, *Billy Joel* , 52.

31. Ibid., 55.

32. Tom Bahler, "An Interview with Tom Bahler," *C'mon Get Happy: The Unofficial Website of the Partridge Family*, n.d., http://www.cmongethappy. com/interviews/tb/tombahler4.html.

33. Bordowitz, *Billy Joel*, 55.

34. Schruers, *Billy Joel*, 78.

35. Ibid., 79.

36. Tim Riley, *Tell Me Why: A Beatles Commentary*, 279.

37. I would like to acknowledge Francis (Frank) MacFarlane (1925–2000) who, in 1979, graciously typed out the lyrics of this song from my handwritten transcription. In the process, he facilitated and encouraged the beginnings of this study. Thanks, Pop.

38. Clark, discussion with the author, June 9, 2014.

39. I struggled for years to find a suitable way to describe "Tomorrow Is Today" and ascertain its source. I remember asking friends what they thought this influence might be, but answers came there none. In addition to the obvious inspiration of the Beatles' "Let It Be," I finally settled on the somewhat obscure precursor of "You'll Never Walk Alone" by Rodgers and Hammerstein. Since there are also a number of blues and jazz elements present in "Tomorrow Is Today," perhaps we could say that Joel's concept here may have been "You'll Never Walk Alone" as it might have been reimagined by Leonard Bernstein for *West Side Story* (1957).

40. Since both songs are in the same key and in the identical position of their respective album sides, the listener could assert that a deeper structural and textual relationship exists between them. Antipodal?

2. THE STREETLIFE SERENADER

1. Childs, "Billy Joel: Piano Man."

2. Ibid.

3. Schruers, *Billy Joel*, 95–96.

4. Clive Davis, *The Soundtrack of My Life*, 144–45.

5. Bordowitz, *Billy Joel*, 62–71.

6. Jerry Burgan with Alan Rifkin, *Wounds to Bind: A Memoir of the Folk-Rock Revolution*, 4–7.

7. Ibid., 197.

8. Ibid., 160.

9. Ibid.

10. Don Evans, discussion with the author, October 2, 2014.

11. Billy Joel, *Songs in the Attic*, Columbia/Family, 1981, LP.

12. Childs, "Billy Joel: Piano Man."

13. It should also be noted that prior to the sessions for *Piano Man* (1973), "The Ballad of Billy the Kid" was frequently performed by Billy Joel in concert. Those performances reveal that the basic arrangement of the song was already in place.

14. Walter Everett, "The Learned vs. the Vernacular in the Songs of Billy Joel," *Contemporary Music Review* 18, no. 4 (2000): 105–29.

15. Phil Ramone, interview by Maureen Droney, November 14, 2008, http:/
/www.artofrecordproduction.com/index.php/asarp-members/full-keynotevide-
os.

16. Evans, discussion with the author, October 2, 2014.

17. Childs, "Billy Joel: Piano Man."

18. Philip Norman, *Elton John: The Definitive Biography*, 504.

19. Evans, discussion with the author, October 2, 2014.

20. This may be why the Face to Face tours of the 1990s and 2000s were so successful. During those shows, Elton John and Billy Joel would play their respective sets back-to-back and then join each other onstage for duets. Viewing these performances, we can see how the differences between the two helped to create and sustain a marvelous chemistry in a live setting.

21. Billy Joel, "Billy Joel Interview 1977," YouTube video, 3:40, 1977, https://youtu.be/AljfNsA6t30.

22. Joel, "In Conversation with Judy Carmichael."

23. Schruers, *Billy Joel*, 104–5.

24. Childs, "Billy Joel: Piano Man."

25. Murray Campbell, "Timbre (i)," *Grove Music Online*, n.d., http://
ezproxy.library.nyu.edu:2619/subscriber/article/grove/music/27973.

26. Jörg Jewanski, "Colour and Music," *Grove Music Online*, n.d., http://
ezproxy.library.nyu.edu:2619/subscriber/article/grove/music/06156.

27. Hugh Davies, "Moog, Robert A.," *Grove Music Online*, n.d., http://
ezproxy.library.nyu.edu:2619/subscriber/article/grove/music/19054.

28. Ira Newborn, discussion with the author, November 20, 2013.

29. Joel, *Songs in the Attic*.

30. Evans, discussion with the author, October 2, 2014.

31. Schruers, *Billy Joel*, 105.

3. I'VE LOVED THESE DAYS

1. Daniel Harrison, "After Sundown: The Beach Boys' Experimental Music," in *Understanding Rock: Essays in Musical Analysis*, edited by John Covach and Graeme Boone, 33–57.

2. James Bennighof, *The Words and Music of Paul Simon*, 181–82.

3. Philip Norman, *Elton John: The Definitive Biography*, 77–79.

4. Burgan and Rifkin, *Wounds to Bind*, 160.

5. Schruers, *Billy Joel*, 112.

6. Dave Marsh, "Billy Joel: The Miracle of 52nd Street," *Rolling Stone*, December 14, 1978, http://www.rollingstone.com/music/features/billy-joel-19781214.

7. Bordowitz, *Billy Joel*, 83.

8. Ken Bielen, *The Words and Music of Billy Joel*, 33.

9. Schruers, *Billy Joel*, 114.

10. Dave Laing, "Martin, Sir George (ii)." *Grove Music Online*, n.d., http://www.oxfordmusiconline.com/subscriber/article/grove/music/47717.

11. Childs, "Billy Joel: Piano Man."

12. Clark, discussion with the author, June 9, 2014.

13. Evans, discussion with the author, October 2, 2014.

14. Joel, "In Conversation with Judy Carmichael."

15. Joel, *Inside the Actors Studio,* episode 6.1.

16. A producer such as Michael Stewart or Phil Ramone might have urged Billy Joel not to sing "New York State of Mind" so much in the manner of Ray Charles. He might have suggested that the track would be more powerful if Joel performed it in his own rich voice. Still, the results are impressive, and have proved to be an enduring part of his legacy.

17. Schruers, *Billy Joel* , 117–18.

18. Billy Joel, "Billy Joel 20/20 Glass Houses Interview," n.d., YouTube video, 19:52, https://youtu.be/PEFR9QeQ4gE.

19. Michael J. Budds, "Schifrin, Lalo," *Grove Music Online*, n.d., http://ezproxy.library.nyu.edu:2619/subscriber/article/grove/music/24853.

20. Andrew Jaffe, "Guaraldi, Vince." *New Grove Dictionary of Jazz*, 2nd ed., *Grove Music Online*, n,d.,http://ezproxy.library.nyu.edu:2619/subscriber/article/grove/music/J180000.

21. In terms of the performances on "Prelude/Angry Young Man," I would be remiss if I neglected to mention that Joel and his new band display an enthusiasm that at times threatens to overwhelm them. There seems, in this new band, to be a general tendency to push the beat. However, this may be due to their genuine excitement about playing together.

22. Joni Mitchell, "1991 Joni Mitchell VH1 Interview: Night Ride Home," YouTube video, 23:08, https://youtu.be/clHPz2TWLmQ.

4. THE STRANGER ON 52ND STREET

1. Bordowitz, *Billy Joel*, 90–91.

2. "Ramone, Phil," *Encyclopedia of Popular Music*, 4th ed. *Oxford Music Online*, n.d., http://www.oxfordmusiconline.com/subscriber/article/epm/22965.

3. Ramone, interview by Maureen Droney, November 14, 2008.

4. Ramone, interview by Maureen Droney, November 14, 2008.

5. Don Evans, in discussion with the author, October 2, 2014.

6. Phil Ramone and Charles L. Granata, *Making Records: The Scenes Behind the Music*, 71–73.

7. Ramone, interview by Maureen Droney, November 14, 2008.

8. Barry Miles and Paul McCartney, *Many Years from Now*, 303–4.

9. Ramone and Granata, *Making Records*, 36.

10. Mark T. Conrad, ed., *The Philosophy of Film Noir*, 1–4.

11. Mark Lewisohn, *The Beatles Recording Sessions*, 72.

12. In keeping with the cinematic theme, one wonders if Mama Leone could possibly be a reference to Italian film director Sergio Leone.

13. It is interesting to consider that both Neil Sedaka's "Laughter in the Rain" and Elton John's "Goodbye Yellow Brick Road" are both written in the same key and feature an identical modulation. In Sedaka's case, the modulation involves both the verse and the chorus, whereas Elton uses it mainly as a transition between verse and chorus.

14. Billy Joel, "Q&A: Have You Ever Rewritten Your Songs?" Berklee College of Music, YouTube video, 4:24, April 1992, https://youtu.be/NJOXOT7ae7o.

15. Ramone, interview by Maureen Droney, November 14, 2008.

16. Lewisohn, *Beatles Recording Sessions*, 138.

17. Richard Buskin, "Classic Tracks: 10cc 'I'm Not In Love,'" *Sound on Sound*, June 2005, http://www.soundonsound.com/sos/jun05/articles/classictracks.htm. (Stewart seems to be referring to the repetition of the starting pitch at the end of the chromatic scale, and thus identifies it as having thirteen pitches.)

18. Schruers, *Billy Joel*, 137.

19. Bordowitz, *Billy Joel*, 98.

20. Ibid., 98–99.

21. Ibid., 99.

22. Ibid., 98.

23. Ramone, interview by Maureen Droney, November 14, 2008.

24. Ramone and Granata, *Making Records*, 37.

25. As noted in chapter 2, Joel's musical choices indicate a preference at the piano for straight eighth notes over triplets.

26. Ramone and Granata, *Making Records*, 37.

27. Joel, "In Conversation with Judy Carmichael."

28. Schruers, *Billy Joel*, 140.

29. Marshall McLuhan and Wilfred Watson, *From Cliché to Archetype*, 204–5.

30. Bennighof, *The Words and Music of Paul Simon*, 1.

31. Interestingly, Billy Joel seems to have been bestowed with all the requisite skills to be a Brill Building songwriter. He could play piano very well, he

could sing very well, and he could write very well. He had everything you need for that job, but unfortunately, he was born at the wrong time. By the mid-1960s, the Brill Building was in decline.

32. Paul Simon, *Paul Simon: Solo*, produced by Mark Steyn, BBC TV, 1990.

33. Ibid. (transcribed by author).

34. Bennighof, *The Words and Music of Paul Simon*, 2.

35. Walter Everett, "Swallowed by a Song: Paul Simon's Crisis of Chromaticism," in *Understanding Rock: Essays in Musical Analysis*, ed. John Covach and Graeme Boone, 113–53.

5. GENRE GAMES

1. Dave Marsh, "Power and Intimacy," *The Compleat Beatles, Volume I (1962–1966)*, edited by Milton Okun (1981), quoted in Riley, *Tell Me Why*, 89.

2. Jimmy Webb, *Tunesmith: Inside the Art of Songwriting*, 15.

3. Billy Joel, liner notes for *Songs in the Attic*, Columbia/Family, 1981, LP.

4. Dominick Maita (musician/engineer), in discussion with the author, August 16, 2015.

5. Schruers, *Billy Joel*, 150.

6. Bordowitz, *Billy Joel*, 145.

7. Schruers, *Billy Joel*, 159–63.

8. Billy Joel, liner notes for *An Innocent Man*, Columbia/Family, 1983, LP.

9. David Matthews (composer/arranger), in discussion with the author, January 6, 2016.

10. Phil Ramone, interview by Maureen Droney, November 14, 2008.

6. FAMOUS LAST WORDS

1. Schruers, *Billy Joel*, 180.

2. *Entertainment Weekly* staff, "Billy Joel Critiques Himself," *Entertainment Weekly*, September 10, 1993, http://www.ew.com/article/1993/09/10/billy-joel-critiques-himself.

3. Schruers, *Billy Joel*, 184. Like "This Night," this song was another that had been inspired by Joel's relationship with Elle Macpherson.

4. Anthony DeCurtis, "The Rolling Stone Interview: Billy Joel," *Rolling Stone*, November 6, 1986, 51.

5. Joel, "In Conversation with Judy Carmichael."

6. Schruers, *Billy Joel*, 186–87.

7. Bordowitz, *Billy Joel*, 162–64.

8. Jones, quoted in Schruers, *Billy Joel*, 199.

9. *Billy Joel: Shades of Grey*, produced by David Horn and Jeff Schock, 1993, VHS.

10. Ibid.

11. Ibid.

12. Schruers, *Billy Joel*, 218–221.

13. *On the Waterfront*, directed by Elia Kazan, 1954/1995, VHS. Dialogue transcribed by author.

14. *Billy Joel: Shades of Grey*.

15. Everett, "Swallowed by a Song," 116.

16. John F. Kennedy, "Remarks at the America's Cup Dinner Given by the Australian Ambassador," September 14, 1962, John F. Kennedy Presidential Library and Museum, http://www.jfklibrary.org/Research/Research-Aids/JFK-Speeches/Americas-Cup-Dinner_19620914.aspx.

17. Marv Goldberg, "'Gloria': A Short History," Marv Goldberg's R&B Notebooks, 2010, http://www.uncamarvy.com/Gloria/gloria.html.

7. FANTASIES, CONCLUSIONS, AND THE GIRL AT THE PARTY

1. Ian MacDonald, *Revolution in the Head: The Beatles' Records and the Sixties*, 328.

2. Bordowitz, *Billy Joel*, 205–6.

3. Gary Graff, "Piano Man Offers His Final Notes for the Pop World," Reuters, August 14, 1997, quoted in Bordowitz, *Billy Joel*, 203.

APPENDIX B

1. The credit discussed here concerns information that has been relatively obscure. Subsequent to this discussion, I located a reference in which Billy Joel himself credits the orchestration to Jimmie Haskell: Childs, Andy. "Billy Joel: Piano Man." *ZigZag*, July 1975. Rock's Backpages. EBSCOhost (accessed January 6, 2016).

APPENDIX C

1. The credit discussed here concerns information that has been relatively obscure. Subsequent to this discussion, I located a reference in which Billy Joel himself credits the orchestration to Jimmie Haskell: Childs, Andy. "Billy Joel: Piano Man." *ZigZag*, July 1975. Rock's Backpages. EBSCOhost (accessed January 6, 2016).

SELECTED READING

BOOKS

Bego, Mark. *Billy Joel: The Biography.* New York: Thunder's Mouth Press, 2007.

———. *Joni Mitchell.* Lanham, Md.: Taylor Trade Publishing, 2005.

Bennighof, James. *The Words and Music of Paul Simon.* Westport, Conn.: Praeger, 2007.

Bielen, Ken. *The Words and Music of Billy Joel.* Oxford: Praeger, 2011.

Bordowitz, Hank. *Billy Joel: The Life and Times of an Angry Young Man.* New York: Billboard Books, 2005.

Burgan, Jerry, with Alan Rifkin. *Wounds to Bind: A Memoir of the Folk-Rock Revolution.* Lanham, Md.: Rowman & Littlefield, 2014.

Conrad, Mark, ed. *The Philosophy of Film Noir.* Lexington: University Press of Kentucky, 2007.

Davis, Clive. *The Soundtrack of My Life.* New York: Simon & Schuster, 2013.

DeCurtis, Anthony. "The Rolling Stone Interview: Billy Joel." *Rolling Stone,* November 6, 1986.

DeMain, Bill. *In Their Own Words: Songwriters Talk about the Creative Process.* Westport, Conn.: Praeger Publishers, 2004.

Everett, Walter. "The Learned vs. the Vernacular in the Songs of Billy Joel." *Contemporary Music Review* 18, no. 4 (2000), 105–29.

———. "Swallowed by a Song: Paul Simon's Crisis of Chromaticism." In *Understanding Rock: Essays in Musical Analysis,* edited by John Covach and Graeme Boone, 113–53. New York: Oxford University Press, 1997.

Harrison, Daniel. "After Sundown: The Beach Boys' Experimental Music." In *Understanding Rock: Essays in Musical Analysis,* edited by John Covach and Graeme Boone, 33–57. New York: Oxford University Press, 1997.

Klosterman, Chuck. *Sex, Drugs, and Cocoa Puffs: A Low Culture Manifesto.* New York: Scribner, 2003.

Lewisohn, Mark. *The Beatles Recording Sessions.* New York: Harmony Books, 1988.

Luftig, Stacey, ed. *The Joni Mitchell Companion: Four Decades of Commentary.* New York: Schirmer, 2000.

MacDonald, Ian. *Revolution in the Head: The Beatles' Records and the Sixties.* London: Vintage, 2008.

Marom, Malka. *Joni Mitchell: In Her Own Words.* Toronto, Ontario: ECW Press, 2014.

McLuhan, Marshall, and Wilfred Watson. *From Cliché to Archetype.* New York: Viking, 1970.

Miles, Barry, and Paul McCartney. *Many Years from Now.* New York: H. Holt, 1997.

Norman, Philip. *Elton John*. New York: Simon & Schuster, 1993.
O'Dell, Denis. *At the Apple's Core: The Beatles from the Inside*. London: Peter Owen, 2002.
Ramone, Phil, and Charles L. Granata. *Making Records: The Scenes behind the Music*. New York: Hyperion, 2007.
Riley, Tim. *Tell Me Why: A Beatles Commentary*. New York: Alfred A. Knopf, 1988.
Schruers, Fred. *Billy Joel: The Definitive Biography*. New York: Crown Publishing, 2014.
Webb, Jimmy. *Tunesmith: Inside the Art of Songwriting*. New York: Hyperion, 1998.

INTERNET SOURCES

Bahler, Tom. "An Interview with Tom Bahler." *C'mon Get Happy: The Unofficial Website of the Partridge Family*, n.d. http://www.cmongethappy.com/interviews/tb/tombahler4.html(accessed January 6, 2016).
"Billboard Aug 15, 1964, p. 5." Google Books.https://books.google.com/books?id=QUUEAAAAMBAJ&pg=PA5&dq=artie+ripp&hl=en&sa=X&ved=0CDQQ6AEwBjhQahUKEwjayPLo4uXIAhVF7R4KHUq8B5c#v=onepage&q=artie%20ripp&f=false(accessed January 6, 2016).
Budds, Michael J. "Schifrin, Lalo." *Grove Music Online*, n.d.http://ezproxy.library.nyu.edu:2619/subscriber/article/grove/music/24853(accessed November 6, 2015).
Buskin, Richard. "Classic Tracks: 10cc 'I'm Not In Love.'" *Sound on Sound*, June 2005.http://www.soundonsound.com/sos/jun05/articles/classictracks.htm(accessed January 6, 2016).
Campbell, Murray. "Timbre (i)." *Grove Music Online*, n.d.http://ezproxy.library.nyu.edu:2619/subscriber/article/grove/music/27973(accessed December 30, 2015).
Childs, Andy. "Billy Joel: Piano Man." *ZigZag*, July 1975. Rock's Backpages. EBSCOhost (accessed January 6, 2016).
Davies, Hugh. "Moog, Robert A." *Grove Music Online*, n.d.http://ezproxy.library.nyu.edu:2619/subscriber/article/grove/music/19054(accessed December 27, 2015).
Entertainment Weekly Staff. "Billy Joel Critiques Himself." *Entertainment Weekly*. September 10, 1993.http://www.ew.com/article/1993/09/10/billy-joel-critiques-himself(accessed January 8, 2016).
Everett, Walter. "Beatles, the." *Grove Music Online*, n.d.http://ezproxy.library.nyu.edu:2611/subscriber/article/grove/music/A2223785(accessed January 6, 2016).
Goldberg, Marv. "'Gloria': A Short History." Marv Goldberg's R&B Notebooks. 2010.http://www.uncamarvy.com/Gloria/gloria.html(accessed January 8, 2016).
Hyde, Bob. "The Kama Sutra/Buddah Records Story." *Both Sides Now Stereo Newsletter*, n.d. http://www.bsnpubs.com/buddah/buddahstory.html(accessed January 6, 2016).
Jaffe, Andrew. "Guaraldi, Vince." *New Grove Dictionary of Jazz*, 2nd ed. *Grove Music Online*, n.d.http://ezproxy.library.nyu.edu:2619/subscriber/article/grove/music/J180000(accessed November 6, 2015).
Jewanski, Jörg. "Colour and Music." *Grove Music Online*, n.d.http://ezproxy.library.nyu.edu:2619/subscriber/article/grove/music/06156(accessed December 30, 2015).
Joel, Billy. "Billy Joel 20/20 Glass Houses Interview," n.d. YouTube video, 19:52.https://youtu.be/PEFR9QeQ4gE(uploaded March 11, 2014).
———. "Billy Joel Interview 1977," YouTube video, 3:40.https://youtu.be/AljfNsA6t30(uploaded December 17, 2015).
———. "In Conversation with Judy Carmichael." *Judy Carmichael's Jazz Inspired*, 2000.http://www.jazzinspired.com/#/billy-joel/(accessed January 6, 2016).
———. "Q&A: Have You Ever Rewritten Your Songs?" Berklee College of Music, April 1992, YouTube video. 4:24.https://youtu.be/NJOXOT7ae7o (uploaded October 22, 2013).
Kennedy, John F. "Remarks at the America's Cup Dinner Given by the Australian Ambassador." John F. Kennedy Presidential Library and Museum, September 14, 1962. http://www.jfklibrary.org/Research/Research-Aids/JFK-Speeches/Americas-Cup-Dinner_19620914.aspx(accessed January 6, 2016).

Laing, Dave. "Martin, Sir George (ii)." *Grove Music Online*, n.d.http://www.oxfordmusiconline.com/subscriber/article/grove/music/47717(accessed January 7, 2016).

Marsh, Dave. "Billy Joel: The Miracle of 52nd Street." *Rolling Stone*, December 14, 1978. http://www.rollingstone.com/music/features/billy-joel-19781214 (accessed January 11, 2016).

Mitchell, Joni. "1991 Joni Mitchell VH1 Interview: Night Ride Home," n.d. YouTube video, 23:08,https://youtu.be/clHPz2TWLmQ(uploaded December 16, 2014).

"Ramone, Phil." *Encyclopedia of Popular Music*, 4th ed. *Oxford Music Online*, n.d.http://www.oxfordmusiconline.com/subscriber/article/epm/22965(accessed January 7, 2016).

Ramone, Phil. Interview by Maureen Droney, November 14, 2008. http://www.artofrecordproduction.com/index.php/asarp-members/full-keynote-videos(accessed January 6, 2016).

Shio. "History of Live Performances by Billy Joel." *Glass Houses*: Billy Joel Web Page, n.d.https://web.archive.org/web/20130116171147/http://www.shio.org/BJ/concerts/#1977(accessed January 6, 2016).

VIDEOGRAPHY

Billy Joel: Shades of Grey. Produced by David Horn and Jeff Schock. Columbia Music Video, 1993. VHS.

Inside the Actors Studio, episode 6.1. Directed by Jeff Wurtz. London: In the Moment Productions, 1999. VHS.

On the Waterfront. Directed by Elia Kazan. 1954. Burbank, CA: Columbia Tristar Home Video, 1995. VHS.

Paul Simon: Solo. Produced by Mark Steyn. BBC TV, 1990.

SELECTED LISTENING

10CC

The Original Soundtrack, Mercury, 1975.

THE BEATLES

Please Please Me, Parlophone, 1963
With the Beatles, Parlophone, 1964
A Hard Day's Night, Parlophone, 1964
Help!, Parlophone, 1965
Rubber Soul, Parlophone, 1965
Revolver, Parlophone, 1966
Sgt. Pepper's Lonely Hearts Club Band, Parlophone, 1967
Magical Mystery Tour, Capitol, 1967
The Beatles, Apple, 1968
Yellow Submarine, Apple 1969
Abbey Road, Apple, 1969
Let It Be, Apple, 1970

BOB DYLAN

Highway 61 Revisited, Columbia, 1965
Blonde on Blonde, Columbia, 1966

SIMON & GARFUNKEL

Bookends, Columbia, 1968
Bridge Over Troubled Water, Columbia, 1970

PAUL SIMON

There Goes Rhymin' Simon, Columbia, 1973
Still Crazy after All These Years, Columbia, 1975
Graceland, Warner Bros, 1986

JONI MITCHELL

Court and Spark, Asylum, 1974
The Hissing of Summer Lawns, Asylum, 1975
Hejira, Asylum, 1976
Don Juan's Reckless Daughter, Asylum, 1977
Mingus, Asylum, 1979

ELTON JOHN

Elton John, Uni, 1970
Tumbleweed Connection, Uni, 1970
Goodbye Yellow Brick Road, MCA, 1973

JACKSON BROWNE

For Everyman, Asylum, 1973
Late for the Sky, Asylum, 1974

STEELY DAN

The Royal Scam, ABC, 1976

Aja, ABC, 1977
Gaucho, ABC, 1980

BILLY JOEL

Cold Spring Harbor, Family Productions/Columbia, 1971
Piano Man, Family Productions/Columbia, 1973
Streetlife Serenade, Family Productions/Columbia, 1974
Turnstiles, Family Productions/Columbia, 1976
The Stranger, Family Productions/Columbia, 1977
52nd Street, Family Productions/Columbia, 1978
Glass Houses, Family Productions/Columbia, 1980
Songs in the Attic, Family Productions/Columbia, 1981
The Nylon Curtain, Family Productions/Columbia, 1982
An Innocent Man, Family Productions/Columbia, 1983
Greatest Hits, Volume I & II, Family Productions/Columbia, 1985
The Bridge, Family Productions/Columbia, 1986
Концерт, Sony BMG, 1987
Storm Front, Columbia, 1989
River of Dreams, Columbia, 1993
Greatest Hits, Volume III, Columbia, 1997
Fantasies & Delusions, Columbia, 2001
My Lives, Sony/BMG, 2005

INDEX

ABOUT THE AUTHOR

Thomas MacFarlane completed his PhD in music composition at New York University in 2005, where he teaches courses in music composition and music research. In his doctoral dissertation, *The Abbey Road Medley: Extended Forms in Popular Music*, he explored the role of recording technology in the compositional style of the Beatles. He subsequently transformed his findings into a book published by Scarecrow Press in 2007. In 2012, he published *The Beatles and McLuhan: Understanding The Electric Age*, a work that employed the ideas of Marshall McLuhan in order to explore the aesthetic implications of multitrack recording. MacFarlane has given presentations and seminars at the University of Leeds, the University of Glamorgan at Cardiff, and the Université Paris–Sorbonne.